Going On With Jesus

Some guideposts along the road

Kevin Smith
with Owen Salter

Sovereign World

Sovereign World Ltd
PO Box 777
Tonbridge
Kent TN11 9XT
England

ISBN 1 85240 112 5

Printed in England by Clays Ltd, St Ives plc.

Foreword

One morning, a few months ago, during the London rush hour, I found myself in a situation that I will never forget as long as I live. I had been to an early morning meeting in the city over breakfast. Now, just when it seemed the world had decided to march across London Bridge on their way to work, I faced the daunting task of heading back in the opposite direction across the river to the railway station. Fighting my way through the thousands of commuters heading towards me rather than being dragged right back where I came from proved to be a very challenging experience.

I've been a Christian since I was a teenager and have discovered that following Jesus can sometimes feel a bit like the day I tried to walk across London Bridge against the flow. I would not swap the years I've followed Jesus for anything but to be honest it's often been hard work and what I've needed most is lots of help and encouragement to keep going in the right direction instead of getting dragged back where I came from.

The work I'm now involved in means that I often have the privilege of seeing people of all ages and backgrounds make the same life-changing decision to follow Jesus that I made when I was 14.

Having been a Christian for over 20 years I know that the step I see them take is just the beginning of the long journey towards Christian maturity that will transform every aspect of their lives. But, sadly at a recent gathering of some 2,000 Christians I asked people to stand if they personally knew of anyone who having taken the step to become a Christian had subsequently fallen away from following Christ and given up going on with Him. A huge number of the audience stood silently in their places – a tragic commentary on the reality that many people give up rather than keep walking with Jesus against the flow.

That's why this book, so aptly entitled *Going On With Jesus*, is such an important resource. Its honest, practical and down-to-earth guidance is exactly what all those who are seeking to keep growing in their Christian faith need. I recommend this book to all those who are looking for honest answers to straight questions and wise advice as they learn to walk forward against the flow.

Steve Chalke
Oasis Trust
London

May 1993

Contents

How to use this book

This book has been produced for people who have just started to discover that knowing Jesus is the most important thing that this world knows. Nothing makes sense apart from what God says about himself, and knowing his Son Jesus is the whole reason for living.

Getting to know Jesus doesn't happen overnight because he won't overwhelm you with himself. He could—after all, he's the great God who made everything! But he loves you too much, so he'll just let you get to know him gently and beautifully.

If you're a person who has just started to walk with Jesus, this book is for you. It is aimed to be something like a street directory, giving direction and guidance for people who are moving into new territory.

It explains things you don't understand and helps you avoid mistakes in travelling around. It's a handy way of learning from people who already know the lay of the land.

ENTERING A NEW WORLD

The Bible explains that Christians are people who have been dramatically transported from the kingdom of darkness (where we have been at home) into the Kingdom of Light—God's Kingdom—where everything is new.

This isn't like moving to a new city; it's more like moving to a whole new *world*. There are lots of things to learn, lots to think about, decide and do. So take time to think and pray about what you read here, and ask God to help you understand.

This book is a sort of 'basic guide' to help you keep moving while you're discovering how to learn directly from God himself and what he's said in the Bible.

THE BIBLE: YOUR GUIDEBOOK

Of course, the Bible is the *real* guidebook for Christians, so you won't be surprised that this book keeps pointing you back to it.

It's important to look up the parts of the Bible referred to (the box at right tells you how to do this) and to consider what God is saying to you through them. A good practice is to write down the things you learn in a notebook, but it's even more important to actually *do* what God desires.

When you first read the Bible, you may find that the way it's written and some of its ideas are not easy to understand. Don't

---

How to look things up in the Bible

The Bible is divided into 66 sections (usually called 'books') and each book is divided into 'chapters'. These chapters are divided again into short 'verses'.

Bible references usually state the name of the book first, followed by the chapter number, then the verse numbers. So, for example, Matthew 1:18-25 means 'the book of Matthew, chapter one, verses 18 to 25'.

Finding the books is easy. Just use the Contents page at the front of your Bible!

(Sometimes you'll find that your version of the Bible uses slightly different words from the version quoted in this book. That's simply because various English Bibles are different translations from Greek and Hebrew, the languages in which the Bible was originally written.)

worry—many people have spent all of their lives studying the Bible and still say there's more in it than they can fully comprehend! The way forward is to ask God to help you understand what *you* need to understand today. He has promised to teach us all we need to know.

The Bible too is like a street directory—there's far more in it than you'll read the first time, but you'll get enough to help you see your way ahead.

WHAT ON EARTH HAVE I DONE?

Now that you've taken a first step to open your life up to Jesus, you're probably wondering what on earth it all means. That's where this book begins—with an explanation of just what happened when you decided to respond to God's call to come back into a relationship with him. (You might wonder why I say 'come back' to God. I'll explain this more fully in Section Two.)

The first Section, **What it means to be rescued by God**, will help you as you begin as a Christian. Another Christian person may well have gone through it with you already. It covers what happens right at the point where your Christian life starts.

Once that is clear, you'll want to know what you need to do next. Section Two, **Understanding your new life**, is aimed to give information on keeping going in the week or so after you become a Christian. Of course, this Section (like this whole book) will be nowhere near as important to you as the Bible in this time.

Section Three, **Things you need to know for walking as a Christian**, tells you some ordinary but important things about everyday living as one of God's children. As you find your way around this material, this Section will eventually become redundant because you'll learn to live it.

You won't need Section Four, **When things seem to go wrong,** until one day you suddenly find yourself struggling with some problem, or you find that another Christian disappoints you and you want to know what to do.

Section Five, **Digging a little deeper**, along with the Special Resource sections, will take you a bit deeper into God's work in you. Finally, Section Six, **Going on with Jesus**, will point you in the right direction to continue growing in your relationship of love and freedom with Jesus.

Of course, the best resource of all for living as a Christian is God himself—what he's like, what he desires, what he wants to say about everything. *He is an active God.* He didn't just create the world and then leave us to it; he's actively involved with us. So you must rely on him. Cry out for help—God promises to hear and act.

Living as part of God's family is always the best place to be!

What did you say?!

One of the things you'll come across early in your new life as a Christian is some pretty unusual language. Some of the words that the Bible and Christians use may not be familiar to you. This book has a listing of many of these words at the back, along with their meanings (see page 145). Use it whenever you need to.

What it means to be rescued by God

 This Section is designed to help you think about what has been happening to you, what you've done and—more importantly—what God has done for you.

Welcome to a whole new life!

Choosing to follow Jesus isn't like changing your socks or buying a new car. It's entering a new and totally life-changing relationship that means you'll never be the same again.

It's only God who can bring you to the place where you begin to recognize him as the Creator and Ruler of everything. Someone else (another Christian perhaps) may have told you about Jesus, but really it is God himself who has been calling you, deep in your spirit, to come back into friendship with him.

When you accept him and respond to his invitation, he makes you his son or daughter. He says in John 1:12:

> *To all who received him [Jesus], to those who believed*
> *in his name, he [God] gave the right to become*
> *children of God.*

Further, he sends the Spirit of Jesus to come and live in you:

> *Peter said, 'Repent and be baptized, every one of you,*
> *in the name of Jesus Christ for the forgiveness of your*
> *sins. And you will receive the gift of the Holy Spirit'*
> *(Acts 2:38. See also Ephesians 3:16-17).*

It's great to be rescued by God!

In the middle of any great change in life, things often happen quickly. This Section will help you stand back and look at what is going on—and encourage you to keep moving!

AGREEING WITH GOD

What is actually involved in being rescued by God? Christians have different ways of expressing it, but it all begins when you decide to agree with God about certain things.

First, you agree that he is God, the Creator and Owner of everything. God claims to be the one who is behind everything that exists (John 1:3). He is the creative genius who decided to make it all. You must believe he exists or you can't come to him.

> *Anyone who comes to him must believe that he exists*
> *and that he rewards those who earnestly seek him*
> *(Hebrews 11:6).*

Second, you agree that you are a responsible person made by him.

When God made men and women he gave them the task of ruling the earth (see Genesis 1:26). This kind of job involves responsibility and authority. Even today we know that if a ruler speaks (a President or a Prime Minister, for example), people take notice. All the newspapers report what they say because their decisions affect us all.

As a ruler on this earth, what *you* say and do matters, too—immensely. In fact, every decision that you make in life is very significant. Your decisions have great impact (see box).

Now God has made it possible for you to decide many things—including whether or not you will obey him. He did this because he wanted you to choose to love him freely, not like a programmed robot. You *can* decide to disobey him, but if you do you are rebelling against him.

We call these actions of rebellion 'sins'. Actually, that is what sin is: because God is the ultimate Owner and Ruler of our world, sin is simply acting in any way that is disobedient to his desires and demands.

But sin is more than just rebellious actions. From your earliest years you've probably found that you often can't stop yourself doing things that are displeasing to God and to others. It's almost as if you've inherited some tendency or power that pushes you in that direction. This power within us we also call sin.

God treats sin seriously because our decisions to disobey

Significant? Me?

If you want to see how significant a person you are, try deciding to drive down the wrong side of the road. You'll quickly find what a big effect your decisions have on the world!

really matter. Rebelling against our Owner and Ruler deeply offends him. The consequences are terrible: the power of sin makes us its prisoners. And worst of all, because of our disobedience, God himself is angry with us.

> Now the holy anger of God is being revealed from
> heaven against all the godlessness and wickedness of
> men who suppress the truth by their wickedness
> (Romans 1:18).

Being rescued by God therefore means agreeing that he is completely right to be offended and angry with you in this way.

God is absolutely perfect and holy, and he made his creation to be perfect and holy, too. He intended it to stay that way. But instead we find the world in a mess because we human beings have decided to disregard God's desires and to act as if we were the ultimate Rulers ourselves.

It's no wonder he's offended!

This rebellion against him leads to deep problems in all our relationships. We find ourselves cut off from God, cut off from other people and even cut off from ourselves.

- Cut off from God. We have a deep in-built desire to know God, yet at the same time a sense of embarrassment being near him because he is perfect, and being near him shows us up for what we are.
- Cut off from each other. We find that others rip us off and we rip them off. It's hard to trust one another, so we keep our distance.
- Cut off from ourselves. We have an uneasy sense that all is not well within us, and we're unhappy with our lives. We don't want to face the realities and results of the things we do.

The Bible has a graphic way of describing this condition; it calls it 'death'. Looking back on what it was like for some of his Christian friends before they came to Jesus, one of the New Testament writers, Paul, said:

You were dead in your transgressions and sins, in
which you used to live when you followed the ways of
the world and of the ruler of the kingdom of the air
[Satan] (Ephesians 2:1-2).

In another place he says bluntly:

For the wages of sin is death (Romans 6:23).

So our position is desperate. The Bible says 'sin, when it
is full-grown, gives birth to death' (James 1:15). If we keep
going the way we have chosen to go, we'll continue down a
spiral that eventually leads to destruction.

We certainly need to be rescued!

This isn't anything new. From the very first, men and
women have rebelled against God. All people have a
heritage which shows up in an inclination to disobey him.
Since the original man and woman sinned, this bias has
been handed on to every person born, and it is very
powerful.

So being rescued by God also means agreeing that you
need to be rescued. This rescue is from two things: (1) God's
rightful (or 'righteous') anger with your disobedience, and
(2) the power of sin that makes you a prisoner.

WHAT'S INVOLVED IN RESCUE FOR YOU?

When a person who can't swim falls off an ocean liner
into the sea, it's
impossible for them
to save themselves.
Someone must go
and rescue them.
And that's exactly
what God does for
us—he offers us
rescue when we
can't do anything

for ourselves. All we have to do is accept his help.

What's involved in accepting God's offer of rescue?

Change your mind. Jesus taught that it is necessary to 'repent'—that is, to completely change your mind about the way you are living.

> *Jesus went into Galilee, proclaiming the good news of God. 'The time has come,' he said. 'The Kingdom of God is near. Repent and believe the good news!'* (Mark 1:14-15).

Repentance means agreeing that the way you're living is not the way the Owner, God, wants, then quite clearly *turning away* from doing what displeases him and *deciding* with your will to do what he desires.

Of course if you make up your mind to repent, it will show in your life! Whatever you are committed to will show up in the way you live, because your decisions matter.

This change of mind involves turning away from your self-centred lifestyle and submitting everything in your life to God. It means obeying him in everything, both in attitude and action. It means you stop living as an independent person and return to the way of life God meant you to live, completely depending on him.

Rely completely on God's action. You can't live out this decision to repent by yourself. In fact, God doesn't ask you to. What you have to do is make the decision—then rely on God to give you the ability or strength you need to live it out.

How he does will often surprise you!

By repenting in this way you are agreeing with God that you need him to forgive you for being a rebel against him. It's important to ask him to do this, and he does.

From this point on you will recognize that it is God's action alone which makes peace between you and him a possibility.

Your new life of obedient friendship with God is established for you, personally and individually, through the death of Jesus the Messiah. God forgives you, but this doesn't mean he wipes away your disobedience and forgets it. Rather, he has allowed Jesus to pay the price that your forgiveness costs.

As I've said, because of your sin—both the power working in you and the disobedient things you've done—the perfect God says, 'You deserve to die'. That is, he judges you guilty. But then he says, 'Even though you're guilty, I've chosen to have mercy on you'. He can do this because the punishment you deserve has been taken by someone else: Jesus (see box).

> **What is God's forgiveness like?**
> God is like a judge in a murder trial who finds the culprit guilty and pronounces the sentence: death. But then, to everyone's surprise, he says, 'But my own son has already died in your place. Your crime has been punished —he took the punishment. So I will have mercy on you. You will live.'

The wages of sin is death, but the gift of God is eternal life through Jesus Christ our Lord (Romans 6:23).

So in a very real way, your response to God's forgiveness relies on the fact that he's chosen to have mercy on you.

And when he's had mercy on you, you're at peace with him again!

Rely on Jesus' death and nothing else to bring this change; it's the only thing that can. The Bible records that it is only through his death that we can be made new. We don't deserve this new life for a moment, but God chooses to give it to us anyway. This is what we mean when we talk about his 'grace' (see Ephesians 2:8-9).

> *If anyone is in Christ, he is a new creation; the old has gone, and the new has come! (2 Corinthians 5:17).*

Do business with God. Before drowning people can be rescued, they have to make up their mind to let themselves be rescued! If they refuse to accept help, they will drown. It's not enough to know the lifesaver can swim well. You have to actually put yourself in his hands to be saved.

In the same way, it's not what you know about God that matters; it is when you *decide to commit yourself to what you know and act on it* that changes will be brought about in your life!

Think about travelling on public transport. You may know very well which bus goes to the city, but getting to the city requires you to act decisively on your knowledge and actually get on the bus. Merely knowing where the bus goes doesn't get you there. It's not until you actively decide to travel on the bus that the reality of where it goes is tested and known by experience to be true.

Similarly, being decisive about the truth of God means making up your mind to trust that what he says is true and then taking whatever action is required. The reality is then tested and known to be true.

HOW DO YOU DO BUSINESS WITH GOD?

If you're going to deal with God, you must deal with him on the basis that *he* lays down. As the Ruler and Owner of everything, he sets the ground rules for all of life. Anyone wanting to deal with him must start off from his viewpoint about things.

His viewpoint is that you need rescue and that he is offering it, through his 'lifesaver', Jesus.

You can accept his rescue simply by praying—that is, by talking to him. Tell him that you agree with what he has said, ask his forgiveness for living disobediently, place your life in his hands and tell him you're deciding to live the way he wants.

Of course, making these decisions doesn't *earn* his forgiveness—nothing you can say or do does that. God simply offers it to you freely. All you're doing is accepting that forgiveness in the way he says it must be accepted.

Once you've done that, as a forgiven person you'll almost certainly want to live the way he says. This is a matter of making up your mind and committing your will, then living on the basis of that decision (trusting him for the power to do so).

You can do all this in the full knowledge that God can be absolutely trusted (see 2 Timothy 2:13). He says he will never reject anyone who comes to him. As Jesus said,

> *All that the Father gives me will come to me, and whoever comes to me I will never drive away (John 6:37. See also Psalm 145:18).*

He will hear you and will accept the words you say. You're acting in faith, trusting the things he has shown you so far and believing what he has said.

He also promises to give you, as a gift, the ability to be able to rely on him, and he delights when you do. Ask him for this faith now. He loves us to do that!

(If you're tempted to think that your prayer is just words

and that words don't matter, remember that God made you to matter. Everything you say is important.)

You might find it hard to even consider talking to God like this. But it isn't. You can talk to him in exactly the same way you would talk to any person you highly respect. He is very great and wonderful, someone to be treated with great awe; but he has commanded you to come and talk with him, so you're not being presumptuous when you do (see 1 Thessalonians 5:17 and Ephesians 6:18).

You may not know what words to use in talking to God. The words of the prayer below may give you some idea of the straightforward way you can deal with him. You will see in this prayer:

- worship and praise to God, in which you affirm the fact that you know he is absolutely wonderful in every way;
- agreement with God about your disobedience and sin ('confession');
- the opportunity to ask him for what you need;
- some action of commitment to him.

> 'Lord God, you are the maker of all things and the judge of all people. I see now that my life as a person made by you has been self-centred and that I have rebelled against you. I admit this and I'm sorry; please forgive me. I desperately want to turn from living like that and live the way you want in everything. Will you give me the power to do that? I ask you to receive me as your child on the basis of the peace that Jesus your Son has made between you and me by his death. I speak to you now in Jesus' name. Amen.'

('Amen' is a traditional way of ending a prayer that means 'I really agree with this'. It's a strong way of saying, 'Yes, after thinking about it carefully, this is really what I want to say'.)

Understanding your new life

 This Section aims to point you to some of the things that every new Christian needs to know and do at the beginning of their relationship with God. (Don't forget to use the word list starting on page 145 if you come across any words you're not familiar with.)

Now that you have decided to follow Jesus, something remarkable has happened. You are now a new person . . . a whole new creation . . . old things have passed away and everything is new with a quality of newness that won't grow old (see 2 Corinthians 5:17).

When you began to follow Jesus you were 'born again' (John 3:1-8). This is not some strange idea but a way of describing an amazing reality, namely, that you have begun to live in the spiritual realm even though you're still living on the earth.

You have been born into God's family and are now a 'redeemed' (or rescued) child of God (see John 1:12-13).

As a new person you will find great joy and satisfaction as you go along in your Christian life. When we come to Jesus he sends his Spirit to live in us. Jesus used a lovely picture to describe this: he said the Spirit would become like a fountain of living water bubbling up from deep inside us (see John 8:37-39).

Of course, being a Christian won't always be easy. As we saw at the start of this book, you have effectively changed sides from the kingdom of darkness to the Kingdom of Light. As Paul describes it:

> *He has rescued us from the dominion of darkness and brought us into the Kingdom of the Son he loves (Colossians 1:13).*

So you can expect that you will encounter some opposition. We'll talk about how to handle this later; for now, just remember that Jesus promised, 'Surely I am with you always, to the very end of the age' (Matthew 28:20). And God has declared, 'I will never leave you or forsake you' (Hebrews 13:5).

Finding peace with God may be costly, but it is wonderfully fulfilling and exciting.

GOD HAS STARTED BUILDING SOMETHING WONDERFUL

While for you this relationship with God is something fresh and new, for God it is really a *re*-newal of the relationship that he meant to have with you in the first place. God made you to be a person he could enjoy and who could enjoy him.

However, right from the very beginning, men and women have chosen to disobey God, with the result that they have been cut off from him. Now, through Jesus, God brings us back into relationship and friendship. In coming back, we understand that what God originally wanted in his relationship with us can start to happen again.

Of course, it doesn't all come about overnight. In fact, we're a bit like ruined buildings—we need total renovation. God has started rebuilding you into something wonderful. You're now a 'Christian under construction'. And he'll go on working on you for a good while to come, until the last dab of paint is eventually put in place and you're completed.

That last dab of God's work in you will be applied just in time for you to meet him face-to-face. In the meantime, God wants you to learn to walk closely with him, to enjoy him and to lovingly serve him.

The New Testament uses different pictures to explain this: the picture of being friends with God (John 15:15); of being children living in relation to their Father (John 1:12-13); of being soldiers following their Commanding Officer (Ephesians 6:10-18); of being servants who work for the best Master in the world (John 12:26).

All of these pictures help us to understand that what God wants us to enjoy is a very intimate friendship with him. (And if you have an intimate friendship with him, you'll find that you also have a lovely relationship with the rest of his children.)

JESUS IS THE FOUNDATION

With any building that's ever built, the foundation is crucial. Paul said that our foundation is Jesus Christ (see 1 Corinthians 3:11). This is really important to understand.

The basis of your very life is God's action. He chose to

make you, and from the moment you were conceived he knew you (see Psalm 8, Psalm 139). In the same way, the whole basis of your new life as a Christian is God's action. He allowed Jesus to die on the cross in your place, and chose you and called you into his family. Any change in your life is a direct result of his action in you, based on Jesus' death on the cross for you.

Fix your mind on this. It's the starting point of your walk as a Christian and will continue to be the basis all the way through your life.

It's also important to realize that it isn't keeping certain laws or doing certain things that makes you acceptable to God. Your acceptance is based only on what God has done and *nothing else.*

Certainly if God has done these wonderful things in you, you'll most probably want to please him. But you won't do this to win his acceptance; you'll do it because you want to express your love for him. Doing what God wants is still important, but now you'll have a different reason for doing it (see box).

> **Pleasing God**
> For a Christian, doing what God wants is like a husband pleasing the wife he loves. If she wants him home at six o'clock for dinner, he makes sure he's home at six—not because he has to obey the rules, but because he loves her and wants to please her.

Rely completely on what Jesus has done and expect to see the outflow of it in your own life. Then you'll be living in the way God wants you to, and this always leads to a sense of peace and well-being.

LET GOD CHANGE YOU

If God is rebuilding you, you'll find your life will certainly change. But don't try to *make* it change. Let him change you.

You'll find that things you've loved and lived for will start to pass away, and things you enjoy and love far more will replace them. And it will surprise you: you'll wonder how you ever appreciated some of the things you once did, because the way you see things will be so different!

You'll discover that the way God changes you will make things that are special to him increasingly part of what you want. He'll grow in you the kind of life he desires, and it will be more and more like the life he lives himself. The Bible calls it 'holiness' (see box).

While Jesus tells us to be holy, you'll find it isn't a matter of *trying* so much as of letting God work in you so that his values become yours. What he wants you to do is cooperate with his work by simply doing whatever he tells you, one moment at a time.

BURN YOUR BRIDGES

Sometimes, when you've been living one way for a long time and God starts to change you, you feel a bit awkward—much as you'd feel if you were learning to use a knife and fork after you'd lived all your life with the monkeys in the jungle. It's easy to think, 'Oh well, I'll just do what I've always done'.

So there's a need, in changing your mind to follow Jesus, to burn your bridges and to firmly decide not to go back.

The decision to trust Jesus is a momentous one. It will impact all of your life. You will never be the same again. There must be no going back, for Jesus told his disciples that a person should not look back but trust him: 'No one who puts his hand to the plough and looks back is fit for service in the Kingdom of God' (Luke 9:62).

It's important to ask God to show you anything about your past life that you should get rid of, or anything that you're still doing that you should stop. Let God show

---

Holiness and cow manure
Someone once explained holiness this way: Imagine that I put a table of cow manure in front of you and said, 'Run your fingers through that'. You wouldn't do it. You'd say, 'No way. That's revolting'. Holiness is beginning to see that things we once thought were okay are really revolting in God's eyes.

you—don't change just to please people! (Even the person who introduced you to Jesus.)

One thing to particularly ask him about is any involvement you've had in areas of life where he says 'Don't go!' We often talk about these as 'occult' areas—things like superstitions, astrology, fortune-telling and witchcraft. Another area is worship of other gods and religions which don't trust Jesus as the true God.

The Bible says that God refuses to share his glory with anything else, and you'll find that you can't follow Jesus fully while these things are still part of your life. It's important to put them behind you by confessing them to God and turning away from them (see box).

If you have any artefacts or equipment associated with this kind of activity, including books, it's a good idea to burn them and get rid of them completely. This declares strongly that you no longer want them to influence your life, and once burnt they won't be able to do that. (If you want further help in dealing with these matters, turn to page 137 of this book.)

Sometimes you'll find one particular part of your life that you just seem powerless to do anything about. Probably this is because you've made a commitment at some time in the past to act in that area in ways that are not godly, and you haven't yet changed your mind about that particular matter.

Such commitments can go on affecting us long after we've made them. And they don't have to be conscious commitments either:

Confessing to God what you've done wrong

One of the loveliest things about trusting Jesus is that God forgives you for your rebellion against him. Nothing is too big or too small to ask God's forgiveness for! Asking and accepting his forgiveness is the first and most important thing to do whenever you become aware of something in your life that displeases God. (For more on how to deal with God about your sin, see page 45.)

sometimes commitments that we've slipped into unconsciously can be the strongest of all!

Paul tells us that we are the captives of whatever we obey (see Romans 6:16). So it's quite common for people to find themselves a prisoner to ideas or actions from the past. You may need to ask someone to help you pray about this—perhaps the person who introduced you to Jesus. Ask God if he wants you to.

Certainly the Bible declares that 'the one who is in you [God] is greater than the one who is in the world [the devil]' (1 John 4:4). So there's no power of any sort that can't be dealt with by the living God!

One important way you can 'burn your bridges' is to openly share with others what God has done in you. Before he became a Christian, the apostle Paul was a young Jewish religious leader who travelled from town to town in the Middle East throwing Christians in prison. Then he met Jesus—and he went straight back into the Jewish synagogues and started to preach about him! The people there were surprised, to say the least! (The story is told in Acts chapter 9.)

KEEP YOUR EYES ON JESUS ALONE

As a new Christian you need to rely on Jesus himself to lead you. Put your trust in him alone. The Bible advises us to run the race of life with 'our eyes fixed on Jesus, the author and perfecter of our faith' (Hebrews 12:2).

Since we are all rebels against God, even the best human beings make mistakes and deliberately do wrong. But though people may fail, Jesus never does.

So rely on him from the very beginning rather than compare yourself with other people.

READ THE BIBLE

If you are going to rely on Jesus to guide you then you need to get to know him well. To do this he has given us the Bible, which is really like a love letter telling us about the wonderful things God has done for us.

In the Bible God shows himself clearly. As we read about how he has dealt with people like you and me, we can see what he desires and what he is like. Of course, this is most clear when God comes to earth in Jesus and actually lives among us. The gospel of John records:

> *So the word of God became a human being and lived*
> *among us. We saw his splendour*
> *(the splendour as of a father's only*
> *son), full of grace and truth (John*
> *1:14, J. B. Phillips' translation).*

So the Bible enables us to understand a lot more about Jesus. What's more, his Spirit also promises to help us understand—not just with our minds but deep inside, in our spirits. So you don't have to be highly educated to get to know him. All you have to do is commit to read what he says and trust his Spirit to make clear what he wants you to know.

It's a good idea to decide to read the Bible regularly, perhaps for a small time each day. It's a big book, and you need to systematically keep reading through it. It's a bit like the painters who paint the Sydney Harbour Bridge; they no sooner reach

Where do you start?
A good place to start reading the Bible is by reading any of the four gospels (the first four books in the New Testament). These are the eyewitness accounts of the people who walked and talked with Jesus on the earth 2,000 years ago. After that there are all sorts of exciting and wonderful accounts of God at work with people!

the end than they're ready to start all over again (see box opposite).

When you read the Bible all the way through, little by little over a long period, you find it's an adventure in discovering God.

BE BAPTIZED IN WATER

The word 'baptism' comes from an ancient Greek word that implied being 'submerged in water'. When people first listened to the early Christian leader Peter preaching the good news about Jesus, they asked what they should do. Peter replied, 'Repent and be baptized, every one of you, in the name of Jesus Christ so that your sins may be forgiven' (Acts 2:38).

Jesus himself left his followers with the words, 'Go and make disciples of all nations, baptizing them in the name of the Father and of the Son and of the Holy Spirit' (Matthew 28:19).

It is right for you, as a new child of God, to be baptized in water in the name of Jesus, or in the name of the Father, Son and Holy Spirit. (Both ways of baptizing are referred to in the Bible).

Just like God's rescue of you, baptism is an action done *to* you. You can't baptize yourself! It's where the spiritual things that God is doing in you are expressed in a physical action. It effectively demonstrates in many ways the amazing changes that God is bringing in your life.

Baptism is a way of sharing with Jesus in his death and coming to life again. It is a washing away of the stain of our sin and rebellion, and a picture that symbolizes the death of our old self-centred life and our coming alive as a whole new person.

But it's more than just a symbol or picture; it's also a place where God works, doing something wonderful that often can only be understood when you look back on it later.

Baptism is an important turning point—a sign of a whole

new beginning in a person's life. It declares that you are
part of God's Kingdom family. Take a few moments to read
Romans 6:1-11, the fullest New Testament picture of
baptism. Then, at your first opportunity, be baptized in
water in obedience to Jesus' command. (Speak to another
Christian who is more experienced than you about this.)

BE FILLED WITH THE SPIRIT

The Bible records that when you changed your mind and
decided to follow Jesus, God's Holy Spirit came to reside in
your life. (Spirits can do that, as anyone who has
encountered evil spirits that have become resident in
people's lives knows all too well!) The Holy Spirit, who is
not evil but wonderfully good, lives in the person who has
trusted Jesus.

When he was on earth, Jesus said that it was important
that he went back to be with God because then his Father
would send the Holy Spirit:

> *I shall ask the Father to give you Someone else to*
> *stand by you, to be with you always. I mean the Spirit*
> *of truth . . . (John 14:16).*

Expect the Spirit to live in you! He will come and make
his home in your body. He is very important for being able
to continue and grow as a Christian.

When the Holy Spirit comes to live in you, he will move
in your life to change you. You can picture him as being like
a person you invite to live in your house. He doesn't force
his ideas on you, but if you invite him to, he'll gladly
rearrange the lounge room, throw out the dead flowers, fix
the broken chair and set the room up just right.
Then—again if you invite him to—he will go on to do the
rest of the house. He's a gentle guest who will never compel
you, but he will do extraordinary things if you let him.

You need to allow the Holy Spirit to literally swamp
every part of your life so that he can give you the power,

ability and special insight that can only come from him.
Paul advised some young Christians not to get drunk on
wine, but to go on being continually filled with the Holy
Spirit (see Ephesians 5:18).

When the Spirit swamps people there is always great effect. Sometimes they feel very excited. When the first Christ-

ians were swamped by the Spirit, they were so exhilarated
that some observers thought they were really drunk (see
Acts 2:13-15)! Other times it seems very ordinary.

The important thing is that you invite him to do his work
in your life *in any way he wants*.

Whenever the Holy Spirit comes you'll see his impact.
When the Holy Spirit came on the first disciples of Jesus,
they found an ability and boldness they'd never known
before.

You can be sure that the Holy Spirit will make available
to you all that you need to be a Christian. This will give you
the stability and bold authority to be able to tell others
about the truth of Jesus.

The Holy Spirit also gives abilities and power to help you do his work. These are often called 'spiritual gifts'. They include speaking in tongues, which is an ability God gives people to speak in a language they haven't learned and don't understand.

If God gives you this gift, don't think it strange, but let God teach you how to use it. 1 Corinthians 14 in the Bible will help you greatly here. It is just one of the many lovely gifts the Father gives to his children so they can do what he wants them to. (We'll look further at these spiritual gifts in Section Five.)

GOD HAS TAKEN EVERY BIT OF YOU

The Bible says that we human beings are amazingly and wonderfully made (see Psalm 139:14), and we certainly know that's true. God has designed you so that you are not just a body but also a 'spirit' and a 'soul' (the word 'soul' refers to your mind, will and emotions). All of these together make a complete person—you. And God always deals with that complete person.

Paul wrote about this to one of the early churches: 'May God himself, the God of peace, sanctify you through and through. May your whole spirit, soul and body be kept blameless at the coming of our Lord Jesus Christ' (1 Thessalonians 5:23).

The Bible teaches that you meet and know God spirit-to-Spirit (see 1 Corinthians 6:17). This means that your spirit and His Spirit come together in the most wonderful closeness. When he shows you something, the way you 'hear' it or 'see' it isn't with your ears or eyes—it's with your spirit. This isn't something unusual, because God has made you to be a spiritual being who can communicate with him.

When you've 'heard' something from God in your spirit, you go on to think about it with your mind, then decide with your will to do something about it. This decision then flows out in action. In other words, God speaks to us in our spirit; we process it in our soul (mind, emotions, will); then we take the necessary action with our body.

Understand that God has taken every bit of you and will work in every area of your life as you let him.

LIVING IN THE PEACE GOD HAS GIVEN YOU

Because God is merciful, he has made it possible for us to know his peace. But his peace is not like the kind of peace we often think of—that is, the absence of hostility and war.

Rather, the idea of God's peace is summed up by the ancient word still used today as a greeting by Jewish people: *shalom*. It's a positive sense of well-being that comes when people know that they are once again friends with God. As Jesus said:

> *Peace I leave with you; my peace I give you. I do not*
> *give to you as the world gives. Do not let your hearts*
> *be troubled and do not be afraid (John 14:27).*

God's peace is a deep sense that we are in the place that was created for us. It will affect your personal life and your relationships with people all around you. You can even live through very difficult times as a Christian person and still know God's peace in your life.

Thank him for his peace, and expect that it will be a growing part of your life. (But don't think that this will mean you won't have trouble or worries! We'll talk more about this later.)

BE CONFIDENT THAT YOU NOW BELONG IN GOD'S FAMILY

The Bible tells us that anyone who has relied on what God has said has always found that he is trustworthy. This is important, because his absolute reliability is the main reason why we can be confident that he has accepted us into his family.

There are three ways in which you can know that you are a Christian.

God has said it. God can be trusted, and he says: 'Whoever believes in the Son has eternal life' (John 3:36). He also says, 'he who has the Son has life; he who does not have the Son of God does not have life' (1 John 5:11-13).

Jesus echoes these words: 'Whoever hears my word and believes him who sent me has eternal life and will not be condemned; he has crossed over from death to life' (John 5:24).

You have believed and put your belief into action by deciding to trust what God says. He promises that you have eternal life. He is no longer angry with you; you and he are friends again, and you will be with him forever!

The evidence of your life as you live it now. You have received God's gift of new life, and as you step out to live the way he says you should, God will bring about the changes in you that he desires.

One example is love: 'We know that we have passed from death to life, because we love our brothers. Anyone who does not love remains in death' (1 John 3:14).

You often only become aware of these changes after they begin to happen! Sometimes someone who knows you well—your mother or your husband or wife—will see it much more clearly than you will. When that happens, be really happy and recognize that God has done it!

An inward sense of belonging to God given by the Holy Spirit. When you know someone loves you, often you know deep inside that it's true even though you can't explain it (actually, you know it in your spirit). In just the same way, the Holy Spirit will give you a sense of sureness that you are known by God. It's hard to put into words, but you *know* it's true.

It's not unlike the sense you have when you're really at one within your family. You just *know* that you belong to them, and you don't need any great argument to prove it.

The New Testament puts it this way:

> *Those who are led by the Spirit of God are sons of God.*
> *For you did not receive a spirit that makes you a slave*
> *again to fear, but you received a Spirit of sonship. And*
> *by him we cry, 'Abba, Father'. The Spirit himself*
> *testifies with our spirit that we are God's children*
> *(Romans 8:14-16).*

'Abba' is an ancient word that means 'Daddy'. The Holy Spirit puts this deep sense of belonging in you, and you know that you're back in God's family where he's always meant you to be.

Things you need to know for walking as a Christian

This Section is a resource for going forward in your life as God's person. It tells you some ordinary but important things about travelling as a Christian.

When you launch out into a new friendship with someone, you need some information about them to be able to build a relationship with them. Further, you need to realize that they have ideas and desires that you must now take into account if they are going to be part of your life. And you also need to recognize that the relationship will be something that keeps on growing over time as you live it out.

All this is true in your new relationship with God.

In particular, getting to know someone well always involves a cost to *you*. Things that they like but you don't will almost certainly become part of your life. So it's a good idea to recognize that there will be this cost before you enter the relationship, and to be prepared to pay it.

Jesus spoke about a man who decided to build a tower: 'Will he not first sit down and estimate the cost to see if he

has enough money to complete it?' (see Luke 14:28-33). He meant that it is very important to understand the cost of following him and to know what he desires of us in our friendship with him.

Having said that, don't forget that in all his dealings with people (and this is very clear in the Bible), God always gives them the gracious gift of making them his children *before* he tells them to do anything. He acted and made the way open for you to be changed by Jesus' death and resurrection. That's his gift. Now he tells you to live out the new life that flows from this gift.

So first he *makes* you a follower of Jesus, then he asks you to *live* like one!

It's always that way with God. *You don't have to make things happen; you only have to live depending on him completely.* (This is not easy for people like us who always want to fix things ourselves!)

Here are some things that I've discovered are important for followers who know they've been rescued and now want to live like it!

MAINTAIN YOUR RELATIONSHIP WITH GOD

Keep your relationship with God active and open. Spend time with him, telling him your cares and happinesses, your fears and defeats. Ask him for what you need. Listen to what he says to you (this involves reading the Bible often) and commit yourself to do whatever he says.

The thing that will most seriously hinder the free flow of your friendship with God is when you sin (that is, disobey God). When this happens, you will often find it hard to spend time with God. It's a little like a child who has disobeyed his parents secretly and then finds he can't happily accept a cuddle from them.

Generally, it's good to deal with any sin or concern as soon as you recognize it. Don't let things sit or drag on. In everyday life, if you owe someone some money, it's a good idea to pay them before you forget. In the same way, get into the habit of keeping short accounts with God!

Confess to God times when you have sinned, either by doing what he says is evil or by *not* doing what he says is good. This can be in your thoughts, words or actions. (The box 'How to deal with God about your sin' on page 45 will help you understand how to do this.)

But as you come to God for forgiveness, don't forget that your relationship with him doesn't depend on whether you've performed well or not. It always depends on the fact that he loves you and has chosen to have mercy on you. So confessing your sin to him is a wonderful thing, because then you experience his forgiveness—every time!

TALK WITH GOD

Begin to take time to pray regularly.

God knows us well, and he knows that as humans we're often slack and choose not to do things that are good for us. So he commands us to pray. He says, 'Pray always' (1 Thessalonians 5:17)—in other words, make prayer a continual and regular part of your life.

Obviously, if you are to grow in your relationship with God, it will be important to spend time with him. This is what prayer is all about. God loves to listen to us (see box).

Sometimes the idea of prayer seems a bit frightening or strange. Often our idea of what prayer is has been formed by poem prayers we learnt as kids or by prayers we've heard read in church.

But basically prayer is expressing clearly to God the things that are on our heart, and listening to him and responding to the things he shows us. Talking to God is a little like talking to anyone you really respect. You carefully express what's on your heart and mind to him. (We'll talk about listening to him in a moment.)

Prayer is a rich time of close communication with God—a time to tell him of your love for him, to ask him for the things you need and to let him shape you into the person he wants you to be.

> **God loves to listen**
> The Bible tells us that 'the prayer of a righteous man is powerful and effective' (James 5:16-18). Jesus once said, 'Ask and it will be given to you; seek and you will find; knock and the door will be opened to you. For everyone who asks receives; he who seeks finds; and to him who knocks, the door will be opened' (Matthew 7:7-8).

Establish a regular time to pray, as the very first Christians did (see Acts 3:1). It's a good idea to arrange this at a particular time each day. Many people find it helpful to pray at the beginning of the day, but you should choose a time that's good for you, when you can be quiet and not interrupted.

Sometimes you won't *feel* like praying, but you can still come to God. Tell him how you feel, then affirm that you will pray anyway, because he has commanded you to. In other words, *decide* to pray even though you don't feel like it. Ask God to forgive you for not wanting to talk to him, then ask him for the ability you need to do so.

WHAT TO PRAY ABOUT

Your prayer will have many aspects. Sometimes you'll just be quiet before God. The Bible tells us, 'Be still and know that I am God' (Psalm 46:10). There will also be a range of things you'll talk to him about. These will include:

Adoring God. 'Adoration' is expressing to God the wonder and excitement and awe we feel when we recognize who he is and what he's done. It's like admiring and praising someone you've learnt to respect highly; but with God it's much more significant because he's the King of all the world.

Adoring God includes remembering the wonderful things he's done for you and praising him that he has made them possible. It includes admiring him just for who he is: the maker of everything (including you), the one who has rescued you and who promises to keep you going, even through the hardest times. On top of that, he's a holy God who one day will judge you, yet at the same time calls you his friend.

Adoration is the purest kind of prayer because it is all for God— there's nothing in it for you. Just as you wouldn't barge into the presence of royalty but would begin to speak respectfully because you recognized who the person is you're talking to, so with God.

Worship him. Tell the Lord that you love him. Think about his greatness . . . his power . . . his majesty and sovereignty . . . his great sacrifice on your behalf! And adore him because the things he promised centuries ago through the Jewish prophets have come to pass in Jesus, and you can know life to the full through him.

Confessing—agreeing with God about your sins. You'll remember I said in Section One that 'sin' is a power working within us, and that this power has been completely broken by Jesus on the cross. God has had mercy on us.

However, there will still be places in your life where you'll decide to do what doesn't please God at all. You need to understand that every sinful action needs to be cleansed by God and turned away from by you. 'If I had cherished sin in my heart,' says the Bible, 'the Lord would not have listened' (Psalm 66:11).

In the original Greek language of the New Testament, the word for 'confession' comes from a root word meaning 'to agree with'. Apply this to prayer. It means to agree with God that the things he says are wrong in your life really *are* wrong.

Something happened yesterday and I called it a slight exaggeration; God calls it a lie! I called it strong language; God calls it swearing! I called it telling the truth about somebody; God calls it gossip! Confession means agreeing with his assessment and asking his forgiveness.

Of course, he loves to forgive:

> *If we walk in the light, as he is in the light, we have*
> *fellowship with one another, and the blood of Jesus, his*
> *Son, purifies us from all sin. If we claim to be without*
> *sin, we deceive ourselves and the truth is not in us. If*
> *we confess our sins, he is faithful and just to forgive*
> *us our sins and purify us from all unrighteousness (1*
> *John 1:7-9).*

When we come to God and ask him for his forgiveness, it's very important that we deal with him carefully. The chart alongside gives seven things to watch out for. It's a good idea to be as thorough as possible in confessing your sin—and of course to be just as thorough in receiving his forgiveness.

Saying thank you. Saying thank you is an important response to a God who gives. When ten lepers were healed by Jesus, only one came back and thanked him. Jesus pointed out that it was important to return and give praise and thanks to God as this man did (see Luke 17:11-19).

You'll find many things to thank God for in your life: The fact that he's changed you and that ahead of you now is a whole new life; the many things he does for you as you walk along with him; answers to other prayers. Thank him for your family, your

HOW TO DEAL WITH GOD ABOUT YOUR SIN

1. Be willing to come to the light.

'. . . whoever lives by the truth comes to the light, so that it may be seen plainly that what he has done has been done through God' (John 3:20-21).

2. Agree with God that your sin is sin.

'He who conceals his sins does not prosper, but whoever confesses and renounces them finds mercy' (Proverbs 28:13).

3. Admit your sin to God accurately and specifically.

'If we confess our sins, he is faithful and just and will forgive us our sins and purify us from all unrighteousness' (1 John 1:9).

4. Claim God's forgiveness and thank him for it.

1 John 1:9

5. Forgive others—including yourself.

'. . . forgive whatever grievances you may have against one another. Forgive as the Lord forgave you' (Colossians 3:13).

6. Renounce the sin.

'. . . renounce your sins by doing what is right' (Daniel 4:27).

7. Claim the power of the Holy Spirit to go on and live!

'For you did not receive a spirit that makes you a slave again to fear, but you received the Spirit of sonship' (Romans 8:15).

work, your friends, your Christian brothers and sisters.
There's a loveliness in being grateful. Paul wrote:

> *Be joyful always; pray continually; give thanks in all*
> *circumstances, for this is God's will for you in Christ*
> *Jesus (1 Thessalonians 5:18).*

Even thank him for difficult situations and suffering that
might come your way, for he promises that 'in all things
God works for the good of those who love him' (Romans
8:28). Sometimes you can't see how God could possibly use
the tough things that happen, but when you look back later
it often becomes crystal clear. (We'll talk more about
suffering later in this Section and in Section Four.)

Relying on God to supply what you need. As the King and
owner of everything, God tells us to ask him and he'll
supply the needs of his people. God is the perfect Father,
and he delights to give good things to his children. He tells
us, 'Ask and you will receive, and your joy will be
complete' (John 16:24).

So it's right to come confidently to God and tell him your
needs as you understand them. Talk to him about everyday
activities, relationships, family, finances, problems, work,
hopes—anything!

> *Do not be anxious about anything, but in everything,*
> *by prayer and petition, with thanksgiving, present*
> *your requests to God (Philippians 4:6).*

But it's important to realize that often God will show you
that what *you* think are your needs are really 'wants'. Your
true needs, as he sees them, may be quite different! Come to
him humbly and sincerely—that is, with an attitude that
says, 'You know what you're doing, Father; you tell me
what I need, because I know your way is always best.'

One of the most important things you can do is to pray
for others and their problems and needs. This is sometimes

called 'intercession'. Often we are able to pray for people who will not or cannot pray for themselves.

God promises to help us understand the things we ought to pray for (see Romans 8:26-27). So expect him to bring people and their needs to mind and ask him to supply them.

This may mean praying for people who live next door to you or others in vastly distant places on the earth. One thing very much on God's heart is that people come to be his friends as you have, so you need to pray for those who really need to know Jesus themselves. Let God guide you about how to do it.

Don't give up. Sometimes you might feel like giving up asking for something. Don't.

When Jesus taught his first disciples to pray, he used a story of a man who kept on pestering his friend for some bread (see Luke 11:1-15). He wanted to encourage us to *keep on* asking, *keep on* seeking, *keep on* knocking (the continuous nature of this action is made clear in the grammar of the original language).

He didn't want us to take prayer too cheaply or give up asking for what we really need.

Rees Howells was a Welsh coal miner who lived early this century. He worked very long hours in the pits but often also spent his nights in prayer. During his lifetime he prayed for many practical things—asking God to change the lives of people around him, or to supply large amounts of money so that he could do the things he believed God wanted done. He found that many, many things happened as a result of his faithful prayer.

Somebody has said, 'More is achieved by prayer than this world dreams of!'

LISTEN TO GOD

God has always had things to say to his people. Through prophets in ancient times and then supremely through

Jesus, his Son, he has made known things that are in his heart.

The man who wrote the letter to the Hebrews in the New Testament said that Jesus, the living 'Word' of God, is God's last word in revealing himself (see Hebrews 1:1-3). In Jesus, all the fullness of God the Father lives. Jesus was able to say, 'He who has seen me has seen the Father' (John 14:9).

God still says that we can hear him speak now. There are a number of ways in which you will listen to God.

Reading the Bible is the first and most important way, because the Bible is where God has shown us what he's like and what he desires of his people. And it's in the Bible that we meet the 'Word' himself, Jesus.

This makes the Bible vitally useful, because it enables us to keep checking the ideas we have about God to see if they're true. In this way, the Bible is a bit like a reference point that will help you make sure that what you think and what people say about God measure up with what God is actually like.

The Bible—God's love-letter. Every time I get a letter from someone I love, I find myself wanting to stop and read it, to read all of it, and to read it over and over again! Because we are people who love Jesus and are part of his family, it's no wonder that the Bible becomes for us more than just a dust-catcher on our shelf.

If you're going to live as a godly person, there's a great need for you to know as much as possible about who God is and what he's shown himself to be like (for he is truth and reality).

Often people approach God and make decisions in ways which *seem* right, based on the little bits of the Bible they know, only to discover later that they weren't the sort of thing God wanted at all. So you need to read *all* the Bible to develop a wide understanding of what God likes and doesn't like (see box).

When we read the whole Bible, we catch a big picture of God that is breathtaking and lovely.

Start reading the Bible today. It's as important to your relationship with God as communicating with the people you love.

God will help you understand. Ask God to help you understand the Bible so that you will learn the important lessons it teaches—and more, so that you will get to know him better through it. This will happen as you soak up the way he has shown himself to many people at different times and in different places.

You'll notice that he is always the same in spite of differences of time and situation. Hebrews 13:8 says, 'Jesus Christ is the same yesterday, today and forever'.

> The story is told of a man who wanted to hear from God, so he opened the Bible at random, closed his eyes and pointed to a verse. It read, 'Judas went and hung himself'. Dissatisfied, he tried another place; this time it said, 'Go and do likewise'. He tried a third time: 'Whatever you do, do quickly.'
>
> You can prove almost anything by the indiscriminate use of verses from the Bible! But if you look at each part in the light of the whole Bible, the story is very different.

Rely mainly on God to help you understand the Bible, not on other people, books, tapes, etc. These things can be helpful, but only if you're first trusting the Holy Spirit to help you understand. Jesus promised he would:

> *But when he, the Spirit of Truth, comes, he will guide*
> *you into all truth. He will not speak on his own; he*
> *will speak only what he hears, and he will tell you*
> *what is yet to come (John 16:13).*

When you know the Bible, God can bring back to your

memory the things he's said and done so you can say appropriate things in various situations—even in places where you are apprehensive because the people you're speaking to disagree with you or are powerful (see what Jesus said in Luke 12:11-12).

Be ready to do whatever he says. 'If you love me you'll do what I want', Jesus said (John 15:10, 15).

If you want to hear God, it's essential to make up your mind *before you even listen* that you will do what he tells you. Otherwise you'll really only be listening with a selective ear, looking for things you'd like to do.

Kings call for obedience from their servants, and our God calls for obedience from us. In fact, Jesus said that this is the way to discover if his teaching is true:

> If anyone chooses to do God's will, he will find out whether my teaching comes from God or whether I speak on my own (John 7:7).

In other words, do it and you'll prove it!

Don't use the Bible to hang your own ideas on. If you want to hear what God wants to say to you, it's important not to drift into the Bible looking for verses or words on which to hang your own latest idea. Then you're likely to simply reinforce your own ideas rather that actually hear what God wants to say.

Great mistakes and distortions of the truth among Christians (sometimes called 'heresies') always seem to come when people read into the Bible things that they want to see there, or when

Things you need to know for walking as a Christian   **51**

one part of what God has said is emphasized far more than others.

Similarly, don't approach the Bible demanding that it answer your questions. It's far more important to allow *it* to ask *you* questions and to challenge *your* life! Actually, what happens is that the One behind the Bible addresses your life. You're listening to God.

Get started now! There are different ways to read the Bible, but the most crucial thing is to make a commitment to start and then to keep on reading.

It's useful to use some sort of approach that will enable you to pick up the Bible's big themes. Then you can study the details in the light of the whole.

If you read four chapters a day you can cover the entire Bible in less than a year. You may feel you're too busy to read four chapters a day, but usually all it takes is getting up half an hour earlier. It really just requires that you make up your mind, plan it into your life and *start*. (**Special Resource 1** on page 119 will give you some more ideas.)

OTHER WAYS THAT GOD SPEAKS

We've said that the Holy Spirit promises to lead us into truth and actually to reveal to us what our Father wants. He does this by speaking directly to us through what God has said in the Bible.

But he can use other ways to speak as well.

Sometimes you may feel he's saying something to you as you listen to a person preaching. Other times someone in a group of Christians may stand up and give a statement or message which they understand comes directly from God (the Bible calls this 'prophecy').*

* When someone speaks a word of prophecy, what happens is that God drops an idea into their spirit, they quickly check it by asking, 'Is this what God is saying?', then, if they sense it is, they speak it out for others to hear and also to assess. If it really is from God, the person bringing the prophecy can expect others to confirm it.

Then again, sometimes people may have specific words that God has shown them that apply to your life (we call them 'words of knowledge'). At yet other times, you may find that something pops into your spirit—perhaps an idea, or some words, or a mental picture—and it just seems compelling.

In each of these situations, it might be God speaking to you. Of course, if it is God speaking, it will be totally in keeping with what he's said in the Bible and it will reflect his character. You'll be left in no doubt that it's just like him to say that sort of thing.

Sometimes God will speak to people through dreams and visions. If you think this has happened to you, it's important to be sure it *is* God speaking. As well as comparing it with the Bible, a good way to check is to share it with an older Christian whom you respect. Again, you'll need to rely on the Holy Spirit to help you understand what these things mean.

CHECK THINGS OUT WELL

From all this you can see how important it is that you know what the Bible teaches. For the Bible is the only really sure way to check whether the things that you sense, or the things that people say, are true, real and godly.

So when you are wondering whether something comes from God, always check it carefully. The starting point is to see whether it is absolutely consistent with what God has shown about himself in the Bible. (If you're not sure and you've only just started to read the Bible, ask God to lead you to someone who has read it a bit more and talk to them about it.)

You also need to ask God to make it very clear to you in your spirit that these things are indeed what he's saying.

As well, you'll often find it helpful to share what you want to check with the little group of Christians you relate to most closely. If God is really showing you something, expect that they will be able to pray and confirm that it's right.

And don't necessarily avoid asking people you think might disagree with you. After all, if God is speaking and people are genuinely listening, even where they don't agree with one another, God can bring them to see the truth!

YOU ARE PART OF THE LIVING CHURCH

When God brings you into his family, he makes you part of his church. This isn't an organisation but an *organism*—that is, a living, vibrant thing made up of millions of people around the world who belong to God just as you do.

You'll probably find there are some other Christians who live near you. The Bible says that God sees you together as his people.

Over the years, the way Christians have lived has been to run organisations called 'churches'. Often several of these exist in the one area.

But it's important to see that 'the church' isn't really any of these organisations. The church is God's family, and you're a member of it because he's put you in it. Any association you then have with particular people or groups doesn't influence your membership in God's church one bit.

So being part of God's church—his people—is not an option. You're in the church whether you like it or not! You need to take the advice of the writer to the Hebrews: 'Let us not give up meeting together, as some are in the habit of doing, but let us encourage one another' (Hebrews 10:25).

Ask God to lead you to the group of Christians he wants

you to be amongst. Don't try and find a perfect group: even if you did, it wouldn't stay perfect once you or I joined!

LOVE AND HONOUR OTHERS

As in any family, in God's family you don't have much choice about who your brothers and sisters are! But if we're all living dependent on God (and not just doing our own thing), it should mean we'll get on well with others in the family.

And as we obey God together, that's exactly what we find happening.

This isn't surprising. If it's true that Christians all have one Father, and that he puts us all together, then we should find that as the children of God we live in love together. Jesus said,

> *A new commandment I give you: love one another. As*
> *I have loved you, so you must love one another. By*
> *this all men will know that you are my disciples, if*
> *you love one another (John 13:34-35).*

The New Testament describes this love as 'submission to one another'. Basically this means that we're to have an attitude to each other that respects and honours each other as the people God says we are, and that we deal with each other in a way that reflects that attitude—both when we agree with each other and when we don't (see box).

Christians are called to live in submission to each other in all relationships. Paul said:

> *Be very careful, then, how you*
> *live—not as unwise but as wise,*
> *making the most of every*
> *opportunity, because the days are*
> *evil . . . Do not get drunk on wine*

> **Honour one another**
> 'Love must be sincere. Hate what is evil; cling to what is good. Be devoted to one another in brotherly love. Honour one another above yourselves' (Roman 12:9-10).

> *. . . Instead be filled with the Spirit . . . Submit to one*
> *another out of reverence for Christ (Ephesians*
> *5:15-21).*

It's important to know that the Bible tells you it's right to honour various people your life: your parents; your husband or wife; your master or slave (your 'boss' or 'employee' in the modern world); those who teach you in the Christian walk; those in authority. (Check out such passages as Ephesians 5:21–6:9; 1 Peter 3:1-7; Romans 13:1-7; 1 Timothy 5:17.)

Honour doesn't rely on people's good performance. We honour each other because God has made us the people we are. For example, a father may be the worst father in the world, but we still honour him as a father because that's what God has made him. And God says there is a blessing for those who honour their father and mother (see Ephesians 6:2-3 and Deuteronomy 5:16).

To lovingly honour one another—which is what true submission is—is very different from being pushed down under some heavy authority. You should never blindly obey any person or rule. That's not submission but submersion.

Submission is being willing to allow God to lead you through others, with great respect for them—while always maintaining your own responsibility to personally discern where God is taking you.

You should expect that God will enable you to be open in your spirit towards others, in a way that can only come when the Holy Spirit gives you the ability.

BE RECONCILED WITH GOD AND OTHERS

Often trade unions have the task of 'conciliating'—that is, getting bosses and workers to agree together. *Re*-conciliation is the idea of bringing together people who used to agree but have had a dispute so that they agree again.

Wherever people have been cut off from others, reconciliation is needed. For us who have been cut off from God—and as a result often also cut off from our neighbours—this reconciliation has been achieved by Jesus.

And not cheaply, either. We can be reconciled with God and others only because God paid the price of sending Jesus into the world to rescue us. Our debt to God has been paid in full, and we who were once rebels against him have been judged guilty and then forgiven.

We are right to be guilty for our rebellion against God, but reconciliation says we are really forgiven. The guilt we've known is removed, which actually changes us, defusing our anger and loneliness and changing us so much that we are free to change our mind about living the way we have. We find ourselves really able to relax with God because we're friends again (see box).

So reconciliation is God's work. It's an action of his grace—we don't deserve it, but he freely and lovingly does it anyway. It doesn't depend on our *feelings* of peace but on the fact that God has made the peace a fact. Your reconciliation is reality, and your feelings will come in line with this as you go along.

(If you still feel guilty, ask God to show you why this is so, because sometimes we can experience false guilt that makes us feel bad even though God has acted wonderfully.)

> **God makes us friends again**
> 'All this is from God, who reconciled us to himself through Christ and gave us the ministry of reconciliation: that God was reconciling the world to himself in Christ, not counting men's sins against them. And he has committed to us the message of reconciliation. We are therefore Christ's ambassadors, as though God were making his appeal through us. We implore you on Christ's behalf: be reconciled to God' (2 Corinthians 5:18-20. See also Romans 5:1, 9-10).

God's reconciliation will enable you to see and deal with others differently. Peace with God will mean peace with others also, including your family and people who live around you (see 1 John 4:7-8, 16-21).

So enjoy the fact that God has forgiven you and you're friends again with him, and expect him to quietly bring changes in the relationships of your life. Don't try and make the changes happen. Just be the person God makes you to be and expect that you'll see changes in your relationships as a consequence.

SET THINGS RIGHT WHERE YOU NEED TO

If there are any places or situations in your life where you have done wrong to others—you may have deceived them or taken things from them or been angry at them or slandered them—you may need to set these things right. But you need to ask God to guide you in doing this, for two reasons.

First, there's no way you can 'buy' your salvation by putting right the things you've done wrong. God forgives you and rescues you in spite of those things. Sometimes it's impossible to pay things back—but God's forgiveness doesn't rely on your ability to set things right. (See Ephesians 2:8-9.)

Second, you need to be careful because sometimes trying to make good a broken relationship can do more harm than good. Going to someone and saying, 'I used to think you were a terrible person, but now God has forgiven me and I don't think that any more' may actually be more hurtful than saying nothing.

Any setting right needs to be done as a loving response to God's justice. Ask him to show you what to do. Don't act in any situation until you know what God wants.

(Read what happened to Zacchaeus, a first century tax collector who met Jesus, in Luke 19:1-10.)

LIVING LIFE IN A WORLD THAT'S STILL AT WAR WITH GOD

God calls his children to live in the world, but it's not always an easy place for us to be. The world is still basically at war with God, and for those who love him, living here is a bit like living in hostile enemy territory!

Jesus says he has chosen us out of the world, but nevertheless still wants us to live here (John 15:19, 17:15-17). One way Christians often express this is to say we are called to live *in* the world but not *of* it (that is, not to live in the world's rebellious way).

So God wants you to go on living amongst your family, your neighbours, your friends—all of whom he's made and says he owns, even when they ignore the fact that he exists. He also wants you to live as part of his rescued family, but it's important that what you do with other Christians doesn't cut you off from other people in your community.

Of course, as you live alongside people in your day-to-day life, you'll need to ask God to guide you—for the kind of people we associate with always influences the kind of people we are. God has made us to learn from each other, and some of this learning is very subtle (no one ever has a formal lesson in how to swear!).

But God doesn't want you to stop being friends with people who aren't Christians. He calls us to relate freely to everyone he's made, just as Jesus did.

In Jesus' day, the religious leaders were shocked that Jesus would associate with socially unacceptable people (see, for example, Matthew 9:9-13). But Jesus himself didn't think it at all strange to be with them. He showed them that they were acceptable to him because they were people that his Father had made.

In fact, when they were with him, such people saw themselves as they really were and understood that their life displeased God, and they asked for God's forgiveness.

God wants us to love others the way he does. This doesn't mean loving everyone the way we love our own family, or even the way we love other Christians; but there is a general love that God gives us for others around us, a love that expresses itself in interest and concern and respect. Trust God to show you specific ways to show love towards those you associate with.

Almost certainly, if you live the new life that God has brought to you, who you are and why you do what you do will come up in conversation. And if you find yourself ready to talk to your friends about Jesus (you may find it a little strange at first), it will indicate that you're quite free to be the person God made you to be with them.

Of course, you must never have a superior attitude to them. After all, as someone said a long time ago, 'There, but for the grace of God, go I'!

DON'T GET SUCKED INTO THE WORLD SYSTEM

Because we still live in the world, the danger is that we'll be sucked into its ways. The Bible strongly speaks against this. Paul wrote to the Roman Christians, 'Don't let the world around you squeeze you into its mould . . .' (Romans 12:2, J. B. Phillips' translation).

James also made a very strong statement about those who say they belong to Christ and yet live lives out of keeping with him. 'Don't you know that friendship with the world is hatred towards God? Anyone who chooses to be a friend of the world becomes an enemy of God' (James 4:4).

> **In the world but protected**
> Jesus prayed: 'My prayer is not that you take them [my followers] out of the world but that you protect them from the evil one. They are not of the world, even as I am not of it. Sanctify them by the truth; your word is truth' (John 17:15-17).

Paul says that the church is to be like a 'bride' for Christ (2 Corinthians 11:2). He uses this picture to show that all Christians together need to be devoted to Jesus in a very strong way.

Jesus prayed that God would protect us as we live in the world, and He does (see box). However, if you want to be devoted to Jesus and at the same time go along with the things the world system wants you to do, you'll find yourself in a very uncomfortable position. Half the time you'll want to do what's pleasing to God, and the other half you'll want to do what the world system tells you.

We talk about this as being 'double-minded'. It usually results in being confused and unable to decide to do many of the things we know we should.

Choosing not to be caught up in the world's system doesn't mean withdrawing from people around us. But as you live among them, God wants you to clearly choose all the time to do what Jesus asks of you as your primary and sole motivating thing.

TELL OTHERS ABOUT YOUR NEW
RELATIONSHIP WITH GOD

When someone gets engaged to be married, they usually find it difficult not to tell others about it! They're excited about the person who has changed their life and is going to change it even more when they get married.

In a similar way, you'll probably find that you want to tell others about the things that have happened in your life as a result of God's action in you. You can expect God to use your relationship with him to help others see him as the lovely person he is.

Speak and live so that God is given all the praise (for he deserves it) and so that people clearly see what a mighty God he is. He wants people to hear about him so that they too will be brought back into his family.

Don't worry if you don't know what to say. God has promised to give you the words you need. Jesus said, 'I will give you words and wisdom that none of your enemies will be able to resist or contradict' (see Luke 21:12-19). Trust him for it!

We see this clearly in the experience of the early Christians.

Just before Jesus went back to live with his Father, he met with his disciples in Jerusalem and said to them: 'You will be my witnesses in Jerusalem, and in all Judea and Samaria, and to the ends of the earth' (Acts 1:8).

A witness is someone who sees or experiences something first-hand—a car accident, say—and can then speak about it confidently. He knows the truth because he was there when it happened.

Those early disciples told people about what they'd seen and heard. They spoke confidently 'in Jesus' name' (that is, they said just what he might have said in the same circumstances).

They certainly didn't stay on the defensive! After Jesus was crucified they were frightened, bewildered people, but a little while later (after God had brought him to life) they became fearless. The fact that they had spent time with Jesus was clearly evident to others (see Acts 4:13).

Christians today often see 'witnessing' as going out specially to find someone to tell them about Jesus. But really, being a witness is much more a matter of living among the people you mix with every day and letting the evidence that Jesus has made you a new person show.

The truth is, you *are* a witness; you don't have to try to make yourself one! Just live out the truth God has shown you, and when you have the opportunity, tell your story as you see it. He'll give you the ability you need for every

situation, and he'll use what you say for his purposes.

Sometimes saying things about Jesus can be uncomfortable, but don't be surprised by this. You're a child of God, and when your Father's values show in you, they will confront a world system which is in rebellion against him.

Jesus used a picture to express this: he said we are like salt and light (see Matthew 5:13-15). Salt and light both have a quiet but strong impact on things.

You should expect that your transformed life will impact the darkness of the world around you.

SUFFERING

You'll probably find that there will be occasions when being a Christian makes for a rough time from other people.

Jesus knew what it was to suffer at the hands of religious and government leaders, and of course he knew what it was to die. And he said that those who followed him could expect their life in this respect to be the same as his:

> *If the world hates you, keep in mind that it hated me first . . . If they persecuted me, they will persecute you also . . . They will treat you this way because of my name (John 15:18-21).*

Some people say that when you become a Christian all your problems are solved, but that's far from accurate. Certainly it's true that God gives you the ability to endure things you could never have thought possible. But he doesn't just instantly take suffering away. It's still a very real and important part of life in a broken world.

In fact, suffering is a reality of all living and growth. As the athletes say, there is rarely gain without pain.

However, don't go and seek pain. Rather, understand that suffering *will* sometimes happen, but God promises that he is fully able to support us in it. Paul said that God once told him, 'My grace is sufficient for you, for my power is made perfect in weakness' (2 Corinthians 12:8). In other words, when you're weak, his strength in you will be more clearly seen.

This will enable you to put up with suffering and recognize that through it God is actually going to build your character. Paul wrote:

> *We . . . rejoice in our sufferings, because we know that suffering produces perseverance; perseverance, character; and character, hope (Romans 5:3-4).*

The Greek word for 'suffering' originally used here is *thlipsis*, which comes from the sound a grape makes when it's squashed! God can use even the most painful, squashing experiences for good.

Suffering can be seen as very unsuccessful, as if in some

way God were letting people down. But we need to realize that God uses even hard things in different ways (often far outside anything we can even consider at the time they happen) to do his lovely work of changing us to be more like his Son.

It's not success but obedience that counts. Once a group of soldiers were told to go and occupy a hill. For several months they held that hill but never saw an enemy soldier. They never fired a shot. They started to feel useless, but as good soldiers they stayed put, obeying orders. Only later did they discover that if they hadn't been there, the enemy would have been able to mount a sneak attack over their hill and possibly win the war.

The important thing is not whether we've appeared successful, but whether we've been obedient to the King.

BE A SERVANT—LIKE JESUS

God's intention has always been for his creatures to live under him as his servants. In fact, you've been saved from sin and transformed so that you can, once again, fulfil your true purpose: to serve the King. You've been saved to serve!

Service is an indispensable part of loving and obeying God. When God gave instructions for living to the people of Israel long ago, he called them to serve:

> And now, O Israel, what does the Lord your God ask
> of you but to fear the Lord your God, to walk in all his
> ways, to love him, to serve the Lord your God with all
> your heart and with all your soul (Deuteronomy
> 10:12).

Jesus taught the disciples the same principle of 'servanthood' when he said:

> The kings of the Gentiles lord it over them; and those
> who exercise authority over them call themselves
> Benefactors. But you are not to be like that. Instead,

the greatest among you should be like the youngest,
and the one who rules like the one who serves. For
who is the greater, the one who is at the table, or the
one who serves? Is it not the one who is at the table?
But I am among you as one who serves (Luke
22:25-27).

In both the way he lived and the things he said, Jesus showed an absolutely different picture of serving. It was summed up well when he took a towel, wrapped it around his waist and washed his disciples' feet—an action which in the culture of his day was the job of a servant.

He then went on to challenge his followers to serve in the same way: 'Now that I, your Lord and Teacher, have washed your feet, you should also wash one another's feet' (John 13:14).

God calls us as servants in his Kingdom to be those who keep looking for what he wants done. It may or may not mean joining an organisation to do some particular thing. But it will certainly mean walking into every situation asking God, 'What would you like me to do here, Lord?'—then doing what he says. And then when you've done it, being prepared to stand by, waiting for his next command.

If you decide *not* to do something he's said, the chances are you won't be ready to receive what he asks you to do next. A faithful servant is one who keeps his eye on his master and listens carefully to him—like a sheepdog and its master (see the box on the next page).

The lovely part about serving this King is that the tasks he gives people always fit really well. His jobs are always appropriate to the person. He never asks you to do what you can't do. In fact, being his servant is the only way to be really free, because we know he'll only ask appropriate things from us.

REALITY VERSUS RELIGION

When Jesus walked on earth, the disciples who walked with him knew the absolute reality of him. They saw and heard and smelled him, and they watched how the things he said were confirmed by the things he did.

Then Jesus went back to be with his Father and sent his Spirit onto the earth—and the early Christians discovered a dynamic way of living with the Person of the Holy Spirit.

But then something began to happen. This dynamic way of life slowly became more and more structured. All sorts of rules were built around it to try to make sure the Christians'

Be a sheepdog
In some ways, a sheepdog is a good picture of what it means to serve God.

A good sheepdog is one that does everything at the

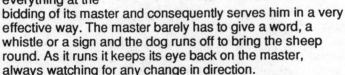

bidding of its master and consequently serves him in a very effective way. The master barely has to give a word, a whistle or a sign and the dog runs off to bring the sheep round. As it runs it keeps its eye back on the master, always watching for any change in direction.

A sheepdog lives its whole life close to its master, keeping about his business and waiting for his next order. It's happy when the master says, 'Go!' and it's happy when the master says, 'Get back and stay still'.

If you've ever watched a sheepdog, you'll have seen how it gets enormous excitement from obeying its master. When he's about to go out and round up some sheep, he gets on his motor bike and the dog jumps on the back before the bike has even started to move, quivering with anticipation, poised to go. A sheepdog doesn't find serving its master onerous.

walk with God wasn't destroyed. But the rules actually took over.

Since then, these rules have tended to prop up people who were not necessarily relying on Jesus at all.

But the real test of living as a Christian isn't keeping religious rules or learning to survive in religious organisations. The real test is seeing God's truth working out in your life.

When you make up your mind to listen carefully to whatever God says and then to do it, you will see the evidence of his action in real effects in your life and the lives of others. You can expect your love for God to flow out in far more than just words or talk.

> *Dear friends, let us love one another, for love comes from God. Everyone who loves has been born of God and knows God. Whoever does not love does not know God, because God is love . . . If anyone says, "I love God," yet hates his brother, he is a liar. For anyone who does not love his brother, whom he has seen, cannot love God, whom he has not seen (1 John 4:7-8, 20).*

'REAL' RELIGION

James, who wrote one of the New Testament letters, said: 'Religion that God our Father accepts as pure and faultless is this: to look after orphans and widows in their distress and to keep oneself from being polluted by the world' (James 1:27).

God cares for all people, and he's especially concerned when they are on the receiving end of other people's wickedness. As you follow Jesus, you will find that loving God invariably increases your concern about other people.

There will be many practical things that God will ask you to do in caring for others. You can expect this sort of thing from God.

However, don't make the mistake of thinking that God is

necessarily calling you to meet a need just because you're aware of it. At different times he will certainly ask you to care for both individuals and groups of people; but you shouldn't then automatically conclude that he wants you to care for *everyone*.

God cares for all people, but that may not be your task as his servant. In fact, by rushing in you may be taking someone else's task. So the important thing is to actually obey him in the particular things he asks you to do.

BE FAITHFUL IN GIVING TO GOD

God is the Owner and Keeper of everything. Everything you have really belongs to him; he's just made you a kind of 'trustee' of it to use it. This applies both to your personal gifts and abilities, and to your material possessions, including money. 'For we brought nothing into the world and we can take nothing out of it' (1 Timothy 6:7).

In Old Testament times, God asked the people of Israel to specially set aside ten per cent of all the things they received. It was to be given to the priests and others who helped them in their relationship with God, and to the poor (Deuteronomy 26:12). They called this their 'tithe' (tithe = one-tenth, or ten per cent).

When people refused to do this and kept everything for themselves, God called them thieves and robbers. They hadn't robbed man; they'd robbed God.

> Will a man rob God? Yet you rob me. But you ask,
> 'How do we rob you?' In tithes and offerings. You are
> under a curse—the whole nation of you—because you
> are robbing me (Malachi 3:8-9).

There's no rule which says we must set apart tithes today. But because we know God asked this of his people Israel, we understand that he's pleased when his children do the same today.

In fact, the New Testament says that Jesus is also a

'priest', but of a higher kind than the Old Testament priests (see Hebrews 7). So it's right to consider giving ten per cent to him in whatever way he tells you to. Or even more, if he says!

Giving to God in this way is really just another means of expressing our love for him. Many people find that they live as well on ninety per cent as on 100 per cent—or better! (See box.)

Often Christians direct their giving through the local group of Christians they're part of, where together they can pray and ask God to guide them about how he wants their money to be used. You'll also find that many other people and organisations make requests and demands for your money.

It's important that you ask God where *he* wants you to give. Sometimes God will tell you to give to a local church or to an organisation that does some particular kind of work for him. But at other times God will tell you to give it to a particular person. In this way God shares resources around his Body.

Be careful of any organisation that tries to get you to give by making you feel guilty about the needs of the world, or about some poor person who's suffering, or about the millions of people who don't know Jesus. It may be appropriate to give to them—but only if God directs, not because you feel guilty.

The important thing is that you ask God where to give your money and then give it faithfully.

> **The joy of giving**
> God has promised to pour out a special blessing on those who faithfully look after their giving to him. ' "Bring the whole tithe into the storehouse, that there may be food in my house. Test me in this," says the Lord Almighty, "and see if I will not throw open the floodgates of heaven and pour out so much blessing that you will not have room enough for it" ' (Malachi 3:10).

When things seem to go wrong

IIII➤ This Section describes some problems you may encounter in living a Christian life and tries to give you some direction in knowing what to do when you come across them.

We live in a world that God made wonderfully well. But as a result of people's disobedience to him, it doesn't always work wonderfully well. So much goes wrong. And even living the Christian life is sometimes difficult.

An American minister was asked one day if he knew any people who had no problems. He said yes, and offered to take the inquirer to see them. They got in the car and drove to the local cemetery!

So don't be surprised to discover that Christians, like everyone else, encounter problems and temptations. The good news is that you have God's assurance that he will use difficulties and struggles to help you grow as his person. Further, God says he won't let you be crushed by temptation.

Remember the words of Paul to the Roman Christians that were mentioned in Section Three: 'We . . . rejoice in our sufferings, because we know that suffering produces perseverance; perseverance, character; and character, hope' (Romans 5:3-4).

In many ways a new Christian is like a newborn baby. A baby doesn't learn to walk, use a spoon or drive a car overnight. Similarly, a new Christian only gradually learns to live in the new way God wants. When a baby is learning to walk he falls over a lot—but through all the falls he learns to be steady on his feet!

So it's not unusual for people who follow Jesus to encounter problems and temptations. Many others have been down that road before you! This Section outlines some things that others have found helpful, and above all points to ways the Bible guides us.

Of course, the most important thing in any situation is to ask God about the way ahead and expect him to show you. He promises never to leave you nor forsake you—and he is trustworthy!

PROBLEMS AND TEMPTATIONS

As a new Christian you're sure to meet trials and temptations. For Jesus, being faithful to God meant struggling with the devil (see Matthew 4:1-11). Ultimately, it meant giving his life on the cross. We can expect that being faithful to God won't always be easy for us either.

The devil—a supernatural being who is evil and opposed to God—is active in the world. He does whatever he can to destroy the beautiful things God is doing to change people, including you. The devil is like the perfect vandal who continually breaks things down.

The Bible calls him our enemy. It warns: 'Be self-controlled and alert. Your enemy the devil prowls around like a roaring lion looking for someone to devour' (1 Peter 5:8-9).

Although he's powerful, however, the devil—or 'Satan' as the Bible also calls him—is not invincible. In fact, Jesus has defeated him forever! As 1 John 3:8 puts it, 'The reason the Son of God appeared was to defeat the devil's work'.

That means we can stand up to the things Satan does to try to trip us up.

James gives this advice: 'Submit yourselves, then, to God. Resist the devil and he will flee from you' (James 4:7). The way you resist Satan is by choosing not to cooperate with any of the things that are his plans.

We'll talk more about this struggle, which is really a kind of spiritual war, in Section Five. For now it's important to see that whatever problems or difficulties we might encounter, the victory of Jesus over Satan provides the basis for finding a way ahead in them.

WHEN YOU SIN AND FAIL

Even after God has accepted you back into his family, you will have times when you fail him—times when you give in to temptation and do something wrong.

Many people who have just responded to Jesus don't understand this. Having done something they know is sinful, they feel that everything is lost and they might as well give up. Sometimes they even think that God has given up on them.

The opposite is the case!

The first thing to understand is that being tempted is not sin. *Giving in* to the temptation is sin. Jesus was tempted just as we are, but he never gave in (see Hebrews 4:15).

Also, while the Bible warns us that we'll be tempted in many ways, it also assures us that with each temptation God will give us a possible way out:

> *No temptation has seized you except what is common*
> *to man. And God is faithful; he will not let you be*
> *tempted beyond what you can bear. But when you are*
> *tempted, he will also provide a way out so that you*
> *can stand up under it (1 Corinthians 10:13).*

If you are tempted or even just confused, call out 'help' to God. He's promised to respond to everyone who calls on him. 'Everyone who calls on the name of the Lord will be saved' (Romans 10:13).

BUT WHAT IF YOU DO SIN?

What if you do give in and sin? Then it's important to remember that God has made a way for you to be forgiven. We talked about it in Section Three (see page 45).

All of us fail. Some failure seems worse than others—and indeed, different failures do have different results in our lives. But in terms of forgiving us, God sees all failure the same. He provided someone who will speak up for us when we sin: Jesus himself (see box).

The most important thing is that with all we are and all we have, we

> **Jesus defends us when we sin**
> John wrote, 'My dear children, I write this to you so that you will not sin. But if anybody does sin, we have one who speaks to the Father in our defence —Jesus Christ, the Righteous One' (1 John 2:1)

turn towards God. Our love must be for him first. As Jesus said, 'Love the Lord your God with all your heart and with all your soul and with all your mind. This is the first and greatest commandment' (Matthew 22:37-38).

If you fail, don't think you have to give up. Read Psalm 51—the cry of a man who stole someone else's wife and murdered her husband, but who went on to do great things as he obeyed God. (The full story is in 2 Samuel 11–12 in the Old Testament).

Whatever you feel when you fail, talk to God about it. Ask him to forgive you, then accept his forgiveness and *get on with living.* This can be hard because we often condemn ourselves, but the Holy Spirit will give you the ability to do it if you ask him.

REBELLION IS DANGEROUS

There's a great difference between committing a sin and living in a condition where you've actually decided to let the power of sin control you. Even as a Christian you can do this.

The first situation, committing a sin, is where you decide, in a given moment, to give in to something that tempts you. But the second, allowing sin to control your life, is where you knowingly and rebelliously decide to live in a way that is contrary to what God desires.

If you have decided to do this, either now or in the past, you are in an extremely dangerous position. A person who chooses to live like this is being a rebel toward God, and God detests rebellion (see 1 Samuel 15:23).

You may feel that this rebellious way of living is something over which you have no control, that it seems automatic. You may also feel it's like a prison which won't let you out.

There is a way ahead. Decide against the sin, humbly come to God for his forgiveness, then ask him to set you free and bring you healing. Be open for God to lead you to an older Christian who can pray with you and help you.

WHEN YOU CAN'T STOP YOURSELF SINNING

Sometimes you may find yourself in a place where you just can't stop yourself doing something wrong. It may be a particular sin that keeps recurring in your life despite your best efforts to stop it.

Usually, as I pointed out in Section Two, the things that you have made commitments to do—whether recently or a long time ago—you will do. If those commitments are rebellious ones against God, they will lead you to rebellious ways of acting.

Further, if you've made a commitment to act in a way that's rebellious, often the Enemy will encourage you to act in that way. Eventually, the combination of your commitments and the Enemy's manipulation will manoeuvre you into a place where you find you have no other way to act.

It's the sort of thing that happens when a person just has one or two drinks of alcohol to help them survive, and after a while discovers that alcohol has become a controlling factor in their lives.

If you find you can't stop yourself doing a particular thing, you need to ask God to show you any place where you've committed to disobey him and consequently given the Enemy the right to control you. (Don't be surprised at what God shows you—it may be something that at first sight appears unrelated to the problem.) Once the Holy Spirit has made this clear, confess to God where you have sinned, receive His forgiveness, then firmly renounce the commitments you've made. Make a new commitment to live in God's way in that area, trusting him for the strength.

Then be sure to deny the Enemy any more power in your life about this matter by commanding him in the name of Jesus to leave you alone.

Sometimes you may find yourself continually doing something wrong because you secretly like it, even though you know God hates it. Then you can find yourself wanting to stop, and not wanting to, both at once.

This is another example of what the Bible calls being 'double-minded'. Until you accept God's view and, regardless of how you feel about it, firmly deal with the sin involved, you won't make any progress.

DEALING WITH FEELINGS

Often our feelings fluctuate after very exciting and wonderful things happen. We can be tempted to wonder whether what went on was really something that mattered or whether we've got it all out of perspective.

The Jewish prophet Elijah suffered a terrible let-down feeling after he'd prayed and God had responded by sending fire from heaven to burn up a sacrifice and show all the people of Israel that he was the true God (see 1 Kings 18:16–19:18). Elijah wanted God to keep speaking to him in the same great and powerful way; but instead God spoke to him through a gentle whisper, put away the feeling of gloom that was smothering the prophet and told him to get on with the other things he had called him to do.

Feelings are an important part of life. God has made us people who are body, soul and spirit, and has given us feelings as a kind of barometer that reports to us how things are with us—whether something is exciting or sad or frightening (see box on next page).

Be really happy that God has given you feelings because they help you to know what's going on inside you. Don't be afraid of them. In particular, enjoy the fact that you can enjoy God. Knowing God is a wonderful experience, and this is something you will often feel in your emotions. And you should. Enjoy it. More importantly, enjoy him.

FEELINGS CHANGE: GOD STAYS THE SAME

Sometimes new Christians find that the sense of excitement and joy they knew when they first began to follow Jesus has subsided. Then they can be tempted to think that God has rejected them, or that they've slid away from his care, or that what they've experienced isn't true.

But being a new person in Christ and knowing God's rescue doesn't depend on how you feel about it. It depends on the fact that God does things well and he can be relied on. Your rescue stands, not on your feelings, but on the action that God has done through Jesus on the cross. He paid the price for your forgiveness. Christ's death makes eternal life yours; all you have to do is accept it!

It's important not to let your feelings rule you or dictate your life. They do help to indicate how things are with us; but they aren't always quick or accurate indicators when it comes to God's dealing with us. They change from day to day for many different reasons.

So if your emotions begin to change, or difficulties come and you start to feel different, place your confidence in what God has done and hold on. You can call out to God. He's always there.

WORRY AND ANXIETY

Sometimes Christians find themselves anxious and worried. Often they're not sure why, but they're not at all confident that they will be able to keep on walking as Christians, or do what Christians do, or be a good example to others of what Christians are like.

Sometimes they get worried about things that have hap-

Feelings—our dashboard lights
In many ways, feelings are like the dashboard lights of a car. Some, like the oil light, warn us when something is wrong. Others, like the turning indicators, show that something is working the way it should. Whenever a light comes on, it's important to ask, 'What is this indicating?'—and to look beyond the light itself to see what's causing it to come on.

Don't make the same mistake as the person who saw the oil light indicating something wrong and took out the globe! Make sure you look and see what lies behind your feelings.

pened in the past, anxious that they will be found out or that they may be too evil to be forgiven. Sometimes their anxiety is connected with relationships or money or some other area of life.

Worry and anxiety usually says that there is some sense of guilt or uneasiness in a person's life. This can take on great importance and affect them in many ways, including making them physically sick.

If you feel guilty about things in the past, God says he will forgive you (see 'Memories of an evil past' on page 87.) If there are places where you just can't stop doing something that's not pleasing to God (perhaps not even pleasing to you), God says there is a way in which you can be released from that (see the comments 'When you can't stop yourself sinning' on page 76).

If you're just not sure that you can survive as a Christian, then you're actually in the wonderful place where you can start to see that Jesus' strength is adequate for your weakness (see 2 Corinthians 12:9-10).

If you find yourself worried or anxious, take the advice of the Bible and trust God to care for you:

> *Do not be anxious about anything, but in everything,*
> *by prayer and petition, with thanksgiving, present*
> *your requests to God. And the peace of God, which*
> *transcends all understanding, will guard your hearts*
> *and your minds in Christ Jesus (Philippians 4:6).*

Of course, it's sometimes not easy to stop worrying! But the more you *decide* to trust God, the more you will find your *ability* to trust him will grow—and the peace that he promises will grow too.

If you find yourself locked into anxiety, it's often a good idea to speak to someone you respect as an older Christian brother or sister who can perhaps help you find God's way through this. Ask God to show you the right person.

If the Son sets you free, you will be free indeed (John 8:36).

DOUBTS

Don't be surprised if you sometimes encounter doubt. As a Christian you'll desire to be truthful and there will be times when doubts push in on you.

Doubts can be many and varied, all the way from a sense of confusion that's based on the fact that we don't know quite what to think, right through to what the Bible calls 'unbelief'. Unbelief is *refusing to believe* what God says is true even though you know it is, and this shows in not living the way you know God wants. God calls unbelief sin.

First, if your doubts are a matter of confusion or unsureness, don't panic! The Enemy delights to make you think that you're the only one who is tempted to doubt. You're not.

The way to tackle any doubt is to stop and see things from God's point of view, and to allow the truth of his perspective to affect you.

For example, Jesus told his disciples that their relationship with him was not their doing: it wasn't so much that they had chosen him but that he had chosen them! God has chosen you, too. Even if you doubt, he hasn't let you go. And he won't! (See John 15:16.)

No matter how *you* feel, *he* is always trustworthy. Stop and reflect on the things he's done in your life so far!

QUESTIONS YOU CAN'T ANSWER
Sometimes you might feel frustrated because there are questions in your mind you can't answer. But remember that you're not perfect yet, so you don't see things perfectly. We don't trust Jesus because we can see it all. The Bible reminds us that at best we see a poor reflection; the day when we'll see clearly is still in the future, when Jesus returns:

> Now we see but a poor reflection; then we shall see
> face to face. Now I know in part; then I shall know
> fully, even as I am fully known (1 Corinthians 13:12).

If you are oppressed by continued doubt, find an older brother or sister who can pray with you and ask God to show you why the doubt is there. You'll often be surprised that the basis of doubt is quite unrelated to the actual doubt itself, and that once you deal with the basis the doubt dissolves. Doubts are often a symptom of other things happening in your life.

If you think your problem is one of unbelief, start off by going to God and asking him to forgive you for that unbelief. Then make up your mind to believe and do what he says, and ask him to help you. (This is exactly what a man did when he was having trouble believing that Jesus could help his suffering son—see Mark 9:24).

Again, if you find this difficult, ask God if he wants you to search out a Christian brother or sister who can pray with you about it.

DISAPPOINTMENTS
Almost certainly you are going to find there will be places in life where you'll be disappointed. But as one of God's people, you'll discover that what seems at first to be a disappointment will often turn out later to be a blessing in disguise.

Paul told his readers: 'And we know that in all things

God works for the good of those who love him' (Romans 8:28) (see box).

It's a serious mistake to become angry or bitter because something that you had your heart set on has failed. If you feel this way, it's important to tell God about it and ask him to forgive you for letting your idea become so important to you. If you don't do this, you may find that you become resentful about people or situations, and that will lead you to disobey God even more.

If any person has wronged you or disappointed you, forgive them quickly and don't attempt to pay them back. You really need to leave such matters in God's hands; as Paul said:

> *Do not repay anyone evil for evil.*
> *Be careful to do what is right in the*
> *eyes of everybody. If it is possible,*
> *as far as it depends on you, live at*
> *peace with everyone (Romans*
> *12:17-18).*

You can trust God absolutely with your life. Thank him that he can be relied on to turn whatever has disappointed you into something that will be just what he wants. He is the Sovereign Lord, the ruler of everything, and he doesn't let anything happen by sheer chance or fate.

CHRISTIANS WILL DISAPPOINT YOU, TOO

Sometimes Christian brothers and sisters will also disappoint you. Even

God works things out

A story from the Old Testament shows how God uses disappointments for good. Joseph was one of twelve brothers, but they were jealous of his favoured status with their father and secretly sold him into slavery. Many years later, after he'd risen to be a governor in Egypt, he was able to save his family from a famine. He said to his brothers: 'You intended to harm me, but God intended it for good to accomplish what is now being done, the saving of many lives' (Genesis 50:20).

Jesus found that his disciples failed, and their failure often disappointed him:

> *From this time many of his disciples turned back and*
> *no longer followed him. 'You do not want to leave too,*
> *do you?' Jesus asked the Twelve. Simon Peter*
> *answered him, 'Lord, to whom shall we go? You have*
> *the words of eternal life. We believe and know that you*
> *are the Holy One of God.' Then Jesus replied, 'Have I*
> *not chosen you, the Twelve? Yet one of you is a devil!'*
> *(He meant Judas, the son of Simon Iscariot, who,*
> *though one of the Twelve, was later to betray him.)*
> *(John 6:66-71)*

You won't, of course, expect other Christians to be perfect, any more than you're perfect yourself! But you may still be badly shaken by the weakness, anger, selfishness and even treachery of some other Christians.

Don't be surprised at this. God has made you part of his family, and when brothers and sisters in a family let each other down it *is* very disappointing.

But remember that you aren't called to be their judge. God alone is their judge. Also remember that all of us in the family have been called to follow Jesus and to serve *him only*—not to please people, no matter how special or loved they may be.

Often if we do things to please people we find that we become confused about who we are really obeying and end up failing to do what God desires of us. Also, those who are 'people-pleasers' often find themselves controlled by the very people they try to please!

Once Paul was in prison and had to face the fact that some other Christian teachers were taking advantage of his situation to further their own ambitions. This could easily have been very hurtful. However, he was concerned about one thing only: that Jesus be obeyed. (See Philippians 1:15-18.)

When your fellow Christians disappoint you, forgive them quickly. Pray for them that God will help them to see what *he* wants them to see. And have a down-to-earth, realistic, humble attitude towards them yourself.

THE IMPORTANCE OF FORGIVING OTHERS

Forgiveness starts with being forgiven by God. Knowing you've been forgiven means you don't have to live with a guilty conscience. God's forgiveness changes our lives.

But we also need to forgive others. God wants us to be ready to forgive at all times, otherwise bitterness can take root in our hearts and grow up to cause a lot of trouble (see Hebrews 12:15).

When someone has sinned against you, whether they ask to be forgiven or not, forgive them freely and without reservation—even if they've sinned against you many times. If someone asks you for forgiveness, you need to be absolutely clear that they know you've forgiven them, both for their sake and for yours.

God, for Christ's sake, has forgiven you for so much that you should forgive others. Jesus told us to pray, 'Forgive us our sins, for we also forgive everyone who sins against us' (Luke 11:4; Matthew 6:12-15).

Again, when Peter asked Jesus, 'How many times shall I forgive my brother when he sins against me? Up to seven times?', Jesus replied, 'Not seven times, but seventy times seven' (Matthew 18:18. See also Luke 17:3-4).

The most important thing to know about forgiving others is that forgiveness is not a feeling. It is an action that you take by using your will—a cold, hard decision that says, 'I choose to forgive that person. I will not hold what they've done against them or mention the offence again—even to myself'.

When you forgive someone in this way, you may not at first *feel* very different about it, and you may be tempted to wonder if you've really forgiven them. But the crucial thing is that you've made the decision. Ask God to help you live it out. He will—he promises that the Holy Spirit will give you the ability and power to do it.

You'll find that in time your feelings will come into line and a whole new attitude towards the person will grow.

WHEN CHRISTIANS DISAGREE

Each Christian is a person who is free as an individual to think and to understand his life before God. Yet at the same time we are a family who have to live quite closely together. This means there will almost certainly be places where we'll have different understandings of things that happen.

There will also be areas where our own ideas get mixed up with what God wants, and this too will cause disagreement.

When we disagree with other Christians, it's crucial that we learn to do so in the context of *respecting* each other. God calls us to respect each other for two reasons: first, because we're all people whom he's made; and second, because

we're all brothers and sisters in one Body who live under one Head—Jesus.

In this Body he calls us to live in harmony with one another. Ephesians 4:2-3 says: 'Be completely humble and gentle; be patient, bearing with one another in love. Make every effort to keep the unity of the Spirit through the bond of peace'.

What we need is such a desire to follow Jesus that we just keep looking at what he wants. If we all have the same desire, even though we may not agree we'll still be seeking the same goal. We won't necessarily just give in to one another, but we will argue with loving care.

Once two of Jesus' disciples, James and John, told him that they wanted to sit in a special place with him. The other disciples got indignant and upset. But Jesus told them all that they weren't to 'lord it over each other' (the way people who didn't know him did). Rather they were to *serve* each other—that is, they were to seek each other's good all the time. He pointed out that even he had come, not to be served, but to serve. (The story is in Mark 10:35-45.)

The real key to handling disagreements among Christians is to keep the attitude of a servant, honouring each other and gently pursuing the truth together.

This is what the Bible means when it says, 'Submit to one another out of reverence for Christ' (Ephesians 5:21). Submission is an attitude that says, 'I respect you and I want to cooperate with you. I come to you with an openness that recognizes either of us could be wrong. We need to discern together what is true and what God wants.'

(**Special Resource 2** goes further into how to deal with disagreements in God's family.)

MEMORIES OF AN EVIL PAST

Many Christians are filled with shame as they remember their evil past. Sometimes it brings them almost to the point of despair.

If this happens to you, don't forget that the blood of Jesus cleanses you from *all* sin—even the most shameful. If God forgives you, you must accept that forgiveness and forgive yourself, and others too. (These are actions you take by using your will. You decide to do them and then trust God through his Spirit to make them reality so that they become your experience.)

If you're aware of evil in your past, it's important to repent, to turn from your sins and decide to do what God desires. When you've repented, you can face life from a fresh new point.

Sometimes it's hard to forgive ourselves, but Paul tells us to forget the things of the past and push on toward the new goal that God has called us to (Philippians 3:14-15). The most wonderful thing about salvation is that God literally remembers our sins no more:

> *I, even I, am he who blots out your transgressions, for*
> *my own sake, and remembers your sins no more*
> *(Isaiah 43:25. See also Jeremiah 31:34).*

If something in your past keeps coming back to haunt you—it could be a fear or an experience or some words that someone once said—don't be alarmed. The Enemy delights to use things from our past to heap guilt on us.

If you've asked God to forgive you then you know you're forgiven. In that case, you can see that the Enemy is accusing you falsely and you should resist him (simply tell him to leave you alone in the name of Jesus). But if you've never specifically repented of the things that keep coming back, it's right to do so and receive God's forgiveness.

You may find that there are areas in your life where you feel oppressed by a spiritual power and need to be free. The good news is that the One who is now at work in your life is greater than any other power:

> *The one who is in you [the Holy Spirit] is greater than the one who is in the world [Satan] (1 John 4:4).*

In fact, everything was created by the One who is at work in you, including all spiritual powers and authorities!

You may feel it would be appropriate to have an older, wiser Christian pray with you about these things. This is often helpful in seeing their power broken so that they don't keep coming back. The first and most important thing is to deal with God about them yourself. Then if he tells you to pray with someone else, do it.

It's especially true that any occult areas we've dabbled in will have a very strong control on our life, and it often requires great wisdom to find God's freedom here. See **Special Resource 3** for further information to help you deal with this area.

LIVING WITH YOUR UNCONVERTED FAMILY AND FRIENDS

Often when someone becomes a follower of Jesus, they find that their enthusiasm and new-found love for him lead them to put pressure on their friends and family to become Christians, too. This can mean that their friends and family start to feel hostile and resentful because it sounds as if the new Christian is saying that he's better than they are.

This isn't true, of course; all of us are the same. We're all people who have rebelled against God and to whom he's stretched out his hand and said, 'Whoever wants to can come and know my forgiveness'. The only difference is that the new Christian has accepted God's invitation.

The best way to encourage your friends and family to trust Jesus is to live your life and allow it to be a demonstration of what God has done. People will make their own observations, and when it's appropriate you can answer their questions. When people see a change taking place in a person's life, often their desire to know a similar sort of change will lead them to seek a relationship with God.

The most important thing to see is that *you* can't change anybody; only God can draw people to himself. He will have to reveal himself to your family and friends, and he wants to. So it's a really good idea to pray for them that God will make himself known to them—and then live your new life so that they see the reality of what God is doing in you.

In the relationship between wives and husbands this is especially important. For example, the apostle Peter wrote:

> *Wives, in the same way be submitted to your husbands so that, if any of them do not believe the word, they may be won over without talk by the behaviour of their wives, when they see the purity and reverence of your lives (1 Peter 3:1-2).*

While it seems to defy human logic, when people do what God requires, the results are what he says too!

Digging a little deeper

 This Section will help you understand more about God and his work in you. You'll notice there are more references to the Bible in this Section. This is to help you look further into the things God has told us about himself. Take time to look them up and think about them.*

WHO IS THIS GOD?

There are many 'gods' in the world, but the *living* God—the God of the Bible—is the one who claims to be the rightful ruler and owner of everything, and nobody can counter his

* Throughout this chapter there are also boxes recommending books you can read to help you go further in your thinking. You can get hold of most of these through Christian bookshops, or borrow them from your Christian friends. (Also note the comments on 'Reading Christian books' on page 114.)

claim! Read what God said to the Old Testament man Job in
Job chapters 38 to 41. God certainly is great!

God is also good. He is a holy God who desires all of his
creation to be holy too. He is rightly angry with those who
have rebelled against him. The thing he wants most for us is
to live in the way he says is true, because he knows he made
us to operate best that way.

God is not just great and good but also absolutely just.
This means he won't overlook our disobedience, and allows
its effect to bring its consequences in our lives. Yet his
justice and love are perfectly balanced so that he is
wonderfully gracious.

We see this graciousness especially in the fact that, even
while we were still rebels, Christ died for us. Paul expressed
it well:

> *You see, at just the right time, when we were still*
> *powerless, Christ died for the ungodly. Very rarely*
> *will anyone die for a righteous man, though for a good*
> *man someone might possibly dare to die. But God*
> *demonstrates his own love for us in this: While we*
> *were still sinners, Christ died for us (Romans 5:6-8).*

Obviously, much more could be said about God. He's
incomparable:

> *'To whom will you compare me? Or who is my*
> *equal?' says the Holy One. Lift your eyes and look to*
> *the heavens. Who created these? He who brings out*
> *the starry host one by one, and calls them each by*
> *name. Because of his great power and mighty*
> *strength, not one of them is missing (Isaiah 40:25-26).*

Many people spend their entire lives studying the things
he's said and done and still feel they've only just begun to
know him. And yet he's shown us enough of himself in different ways for us to be able to recognize him and his action
in the world.

Paul tells us that there's enough evidence in creation itself to validate God's claims (see Romans 1:20). Certainly, in their heart of hearts, most people know he's there. Men and women throughout all history have had a hungering to know a spiritual being like this One.

Paul once met some clever and very religious people in Greece (see Acts 17:16-34). In amongst all their shrines to different gods, they had one marked 'To an Unknown God'. With all the gods they were trying to worship, there was one that they understood was there but didn't know about. Paul explained that the God of Jesus was the one they were looking for.

> **Want to know more?**
> A good book to help you dig deeper into who God is and what He's like is *Knowing God* by J. I. Packer (published by Hodder and Stoughton).

You'll find that the rest of your life is an exciting time of discovering more and more about him, and how his claims are confirmed in the things he does in your life.

THREE GODS OR ONE?

Our God is a great and mighty God, bigger than we can ever fully understand. Although we know we're made in his image, and therefore there are ways in which we're like him, we know he's not limited as we are.

Our knowledge of God depends entirely on what he's made known about himself. As men and women have got to know him over many centuries, he's shown them first that he's a great King and Father, a Being of a different realm from anything else that we know—the creative genius who made and sustains everything.

But this great King didn't just make the world and leave it to itself. In his goodness, he came among us in the limitation of being a person who lived and walked on the earth. As the unique 'Son of God' (Mark 1:1), Jesus in first century Palestine was God in human form. When we look at him, we see what God is like; as Jesus himself said, 'Anyone who has seen me has seen the Father' (John 14:9).

Then, when Jesus went away from the earth, he sent in his place the Holy Spirit, who is also God at work among us. In fact, he is God come to make his home in us! (See Ephesians 3:17.)

We, in our limited fashion, understand our encounter with the living God in all these terms—as Father, Son and Holy Spirit. But we don't want to think of God in a 'bitsy' way, so we have to understand that God is all these things, all the time, all together. In fact, the Bible tells us that there is the deepest possible friendship and communion between the Father and the Son and the Spirit, in a relationship that has been going on forever.

This understanding of God is what Christians usually call 'the Trinity'. 'Trinity' means that God is a 'three-in-one' Person. You won't find the word 'Trinity' in the Bible, but what you will find there is a clear picture that there is one God, yet the Father, the Son and the Holy Spirit are all him.

WHO IS JESUS CHRIST?

John, in his record of Jesus' life, speaks of Jesus as 'the Word of God' (John 1:1). This means that Jesus came as a full expression of all that God is like. Paul said the same thing in different words:

> He is the image of the invisible God . . . in Christ all
> the fullness of the Deity [God] lives in bodily form
> (Colossians 1:15, 2:9).

John also tells us that Jesus came to earth and lived

among us—or, as the Greek language of the New Testament says, 'pitched his tent' here.

> *The Word became flesh and lived for a while among*
> *us. We have seen his glory, the glory of the one and*
> *only Son, who came from the Father, full of grace and*
> *truth (John 1:14).*

Jesus was both a man and God at the very same time. The people who walked with him gradually came to realize that he was the Son of God in a unique way.

Looking back now, it's easy to see that everything we know about Jesus—from the way he was born to the way he went back to be at the right hand of his Father—underlines his uniqueness and his special relationship with his Father. In fact, many years before, prophets like Isaiah, who heard God clearly, told the Jewish people that just such a person would come:

> *For to us a child is born,*
> *to us a son is given,*
> *and the government will be on his shoulders.*
> *And he will be called*
> *Wonderful Counsellor, Mighty God,*
> *Everlasting Father, Prince of Peace (Isaiah 9:6).*

History records how this Jesus died on a cross at the hands of Roman soldiers and how he came alive again. But his death wasn't just an ordinary execution. Peter wrote:

> *For Christ died for sins once for all, the righteous for*
> *the unrighteous, to bring you to God (1 Peter 3:18).*

This Jesus who rose from the dead is alive today! God has made him the Lord, the one who is the true Master and authoritative Ruler in heaven and on the earth (see Acts 2:32-36). This too was something the Old Testament prophets foresaw:

*In my vision at night I looked and there before me was
one like a son of man . . . He approached the Ancient
of Days [God] and . . . was given authority, glory and
sovereign power; all peoples, nations and men of every
language worshipped him . . . His Kingdom is one that
will never be destroyed (Daniel 7:13-14).*

Jesus certainly deserves our obedience!

Yet although he is the rightful ruler, Jesus doesn't want
people to obey him because they have to, but because they
love him. Actually, he said that one of the signs that they
loved him would be that they were prepared to do what he
said (see John 14:15, 23-24).

But he went even further than this; he called those who
did what he wanted his friends. 'I no longer call you just
servants . . . Instead, I have called you
friends' (John 15:15). Friends of Jesus.
Friends of God.

It's through Jesus coming to earth
that God has made it possible for
people to experience his rescue and
the wholeness that he meant for us.
Jesus died on the cross in our place to
pay the cost necessary to redeem us.

One helpful way of thinking about
what Jesus has done for us is to think
of him as a *prophet*, a *priest* and a *king*.
He's acted as a prophet who makes
clear to us all the things that God
wants us to know about himself; a
priest who sits now at God's right
hand where he continually speaks to
God on our behalf; and a king, the
ruler of all, who needs to be obeyed.

Jesus is going to return to this earth
one day, and at that point 'every knee

**Want to know
more?**
If you really want to
get to know Jesus
better, pick up a
modern translation
of the Bible (like the
Living Bible) and
read one of the
gospels straight
through. Simply note
how Jesus meets
people. You'll find
yourself
overwhelmed. Look
at his loveliness,
what he says to
people, how he
treats them. Get to
know him.

shall bow and every tongue confess' that he is the rightful
Ruler (see Philippians 1:9-11). Those who are still rebels at
that time will bow in fear, but those who have trusted him
will bow in love and excitement, because they'll know that
their salvation is complete at last.

WHO IS THE HOLY SPIRIT?

Before Jesus left the earth, he promised to send the Holy
Spirit as one who would walk 'alongside us'. He enables us
to know what God wants, and does for us everything that
God wants to do (John 16:7-15; 2 Corinthians 3:17).

This isn't a new task for the Holy Spirit. Long before, he
was God's agent in creation and in the work of the prophets
(see Genesis 1:2; Ezekiel 37:1; 2 Peter 1:20-21). In the same
way, he was God's agent to bring about the birth of Jesus
(see Luke 1:35). The Bible tells us that his work is always to
draw attention to Jesus.

After Jesus had returned to his Father, his promise was
fulfilled, and God gave the Spirit to his people in a new and
exciting way. At the Jewish festival of Pentecost in
Jerusalem, some fifty days after Jesus had risen from the
dead, the Holy Spirit came in power on the disciples (see
Acts chapter 2).

The Holy Spirit's coming was like a complete immersing
in power and abilities and insight and perception that the
disciples had never known before. This swamping with the
Spirit revolutionized them from being a bunch of scared,
bewildered people into a bold and confident group of
convinced preachers, teachers and helpers.

Today the Holy Spirit is the one who enables us to see
that we need to know God (John 3:3-5). He's also the one
who shows us when we've sinned against him (John 16:8-9).
He works in us to make us more and more the way God
wants us to be (2 Corinthians 3:17-18).

The New Testament says he is like the deposit that a
person puts down when they're buying a car—the first

payment promising that the rest will come later (see Ephesians 1:13-14). He is God's deposit in our life.

The Holy Spirit is still God's agent today, growing his lovely qualities (or 'fruit') in our lives, equipping his people for service with special gifts and abilities, and bringing about wholeness and maturity in his church. But as a gentle guest, he doesn't force his way into our lives. He waits for us to cooperatively welcome him and allow him room to move.

> **Want to know more?**
> A good book on the Holy Spirit and his work in our lives is *I believe in the Holy Spirit* by Michael Green (published by Hodder and Stoughton).

THE FRUIT OF GOD'S SPIRIT GROWING IN YOU

When you started as a Christian, the Bible records that the Spirit of God gave life to your spirit, which before was dead to God (see Romans 8:10). Paul says that the Spirit lives in you:

> *Your body is a temple of the Holy Spirit, who is in you, whom you have received from God (1 Corinthians 6:19).*

What God really wants is for you to live in total submission to him by being controlled by his Spirit. This doesn't mean giving up your own will and becoming like a robot, but rather bringing your will in line with his will because you recognize that his way is always best.

> *You, however, are controlled not by the sinful nature but by the Spirit, if the Spirit of God lives in you (Romans 8:9).*

Invite the Holy Spirit to take control of your whole life. When you do this, the evidence of God's work in you grows. You are able to say no to the things that you know are displeasing to God in a way you've never been able to before. This power doesn't come from you, but from the Holy Spirit within you (see Romans 8:13).

Real evidence of God's work in you is in the appearance of what the Bible calls 'the fruit of the Holy Spirit'. Paul puts it this way in his letter to the church in Galatia:

> *But the fruit of the Spirit is love, joy, peace, patience, kindness, goodness, faithfulness, gentleness and self-control. Against such things there is no law (Galatians 5:22).*

Love. The English word 'love' can mean many things. In ancient Greek there were four words for love:

- *Eros*, which meant the love between a man and a woman.
- *Philia*, the warm love people felt for their nearest and dearest—their family and friends.
- *Storge*, which meant affection and was specially used of the love between parents and children.
- *Agape*, a word the early Christians made their own. It meant loving by seeking the best for someone—whether they loved you in return or not.

This is the sort of love that we see in God himself. He loves us, not because we perform well, but because he is committed to us in a deep way for our loving care, to seek our good.

And this is the sort of love the Spirit produces in us. It means that no matter what a person may do to us by way of insult or injury or humiliation, we will never seek anything else but his highest good.

Joy. This Greek word (*chara*) most often described the kind of joy which is based in knowing God by faith. It's not the joy that comes from earthly thrills or cheap triumphs; still less is it the joy that comes from triumphing over someone else in rivalry or competition.

It is a deep happiness which God works in us and which no one can take from us. It is the awareness that the centre of our life is located in the right place.

Peace. In the everyday Greek culture of New Testament times, this word (*eirene*) described the tranquillity and serenity which a country enjoyed under the rule of a good emperor. It also meant the good order of a town or village.

Usually in the New Testament, *eirene* stands for the Hebrew word *shalom*, which means not just freedom from trouble but everything that makes for a person's highest good. It means the serenity of heart which comes from realising that our lives are in God's hands.

Patience. Generally speaking, this word (*makrothumia*) was not used of patience in regard to things or events, but of patience in regard to people. John Chrysostom, a Christian in the fourth century, said it was the grace of the man who could revenge himself but refuses to, or of the man who is slow to get angry.

This is the attitude of God towards us. If God had been like one of us, he would have wiped out this world long ago; but he has that patience which goes on bearing with all our sinning and will not throw us away.

The Spirit grows in us patience to

deal with others the way God deals with us.

Kindness. This is a practical, action-centred type of care. It shows itself in real things—not just nice thoughts. It is goodness fleshed out in kind action.

Goodness. This is a kind of open-hearted generosity. The Greek word (*agathosune*) was used to describe wine which had become mellow with age. The Spirit grows a goodness in us which at one and the same time can be kind and strong.

Faithfulness. This is the quality of a person who may be depended on as God can be depended on. A person who is rock-like in their reliability.

Gentle humility. This is a meekness like that of a horse that has been properly broken in—its spirit is still strong but it is now under the control of its master. A humble person is someone who has come to a place of putting others before themselves. They are teachable, considerate and willingly submitted to what God desires.

Self-control. A person who is self-controlled is someone who has mastered his desires and love of pleasure so they don't control him but take their rightful place in his life. The Greek word (*egkrateia*) was used of the way an athlete disciplines his body (1 Corinthians 9:25) and of the Christian's healthy mastery of sex (1 Corinthians 7:9).

It is the virtue which makes a person so in control of himself that he is fit to be the servant of others.

HOW THESE FRUIT GROW

The Holy Spirit delights to find someone who loves God enough to allow him to bring these lovely qualities in them. When you have the fruit of the Spirit growing in you, you are really becoming more and more like Jesus.

These attributes grow in any Christian person who will cooperate with God. They're not something we can make happen ourselves. They're God's action that comes about quietly and slowly in our lives.

THE GIFTS OF THE GOD'S SPIRIT EXPRESSED THROUGH YOU

Where the fruit of the Spirit are qualities of character, the gifts of the Spirit are powers and abilities given to Christian people to enable them to do what God wants them to do in his service. Like the scaffolding and tools used to build a house, they're the equipment he supplies so that his church will be built.

Michael Harper, a British writer, has described them this way: 'Spiritual gifts are certain powers given to men [and women] by the Holy Spirit and freely bestowed and manifested through our natural faculties (mind, mouth, hands, etc.) in the service of others, for their blessing and God's glory.'

Spiritual gifts are never meant to make people feel proud or better than others. Rather, they're given for us to use to encourage one another in our life and faith.

It's important to realize that, while God offers these gifts, we must take hold of them. They don't appear 'automatically' like the fruit. I know a young man who became a Christian and then faced the question of how he would handle a dishonest activity in his work place. He claimed the gift of the 'word of wisdom' and made the suggestion that came into his mind. He was amazed to see how God had given him a wonderfully wise way of confronting the problem.

He had discovered that the abilities of the Spirit don't just 'drop' on us. We need to take hold of them in faith and cooperate with the Spirit in doing what he wants.

Sometimes when we ask God for his enabling, we find we can do what he desires in ways that surprise us. This is because God gives the gift of being able to do that thing. For instance, God gives someone the gift of faith, and they find they are able to rely on him in ways they would never have

thought possible. (This gift is always very needed amongst God's people.)

You may find that some Christians strongly emphasize the gift of being able to pray in a language that they've never learnt (sometimes called the gift of 'speaking in tongues'). And certainly this gift has been very helpful for many people in being able to pray when words fail them.

But really, *all* the gifts of the Holy Spirit are vitally important for growing the church. Take some time to read 1 Corinthians 12, Romans 12 and Ephesians 4 to see what the Bible says about them.

SPIRITUAL WARFARE

We know that God is Spirit, and that those who want to really worship him have to worship him 'in spirit and in truth' (John 4:23). But what many people don't realize is that human beings are spirit, too.

God shows us quite clearly in the Bible that the world is far more than just a physical place. Further, people are more than just physical beings. We actually belong to two worlds at once—the physical world and the spiritual world. And what we experience in each world influences the other.

The Bible also teaches that in the spiritual world there is a force at war with God. As God is Spirit, so this enemy is spirit. The Bible calls him 'Satan' or 'the devil'. Once he was a beautiful creature that God made, but he turned away from God and now opposes him with great hatred.

Now because we are spiritual beings, we too are caught up in this spiritual war—whether we like it or not. We can't avoid it. Paul described it this way:

> *For our struggle is not against flesh and blood, but*
> *against the rulers, against the authorities, against the*
> *powers of this dark world and against the spiritual*
> *forces of evil in heavenly places (Ephesians 6:12).*

It's not surprising, then, that we find it difficult to live as Christians. When we decide to follow Jesus as our King, Satan immediately sees us as being on the other side. For us that means a level of spiritual warfare.

The good news, however, is that God has already won the war! Satan was defeated when Jesus died on the cross and broke the power of sin and death and demonic beings (see 1 Corinthians 15:55-57; Colossians 2:15). The New Testament says, 'The reason the Son of God appeared was to destroy the devil's work' (1 John 3:8)—and that's exactly what he's done! It's clear that Satan's days are numbered.

What does this mean for us? It means that we're like people living in a battle zone, still being bombarded by an enemy who won't accept defeat even though he's beaten. Satan's troops are still holding out. But their ultimate end is certain.

In this situation, our task is to stand firm against Satan's attacks and to hold our ground:

> *Therefore put on the whole armour of God, so that*
> *when the day of evil comes, you may be able to stand*
> *your ground, and after you have done everything, to*
> *stand (Ephesians 6:13).*

'Standing' means living our lives on the basis of what

Jesus has done, and keeping our heads down so that we're not good targets for the Enemy's sniper attacks.

One day, when Jesus comes back again, the Enemy will be flushed out for good. *Then* things will certainly change on the earth!

THE ARMOUR OF GOD

God promises to give us everything we need to stand firm. First of all, he makes us confident of the fact that he's won. This is most clearly seen in

> **Want to know more?**
> A good introductory book on spiritual warfare is *Explaining Spiritual Warfare* by Ed Roebert (published by Sovereign World).

the fact that he's brought us back into his family, away from the Enemy's side.

But then he also gives us equipment to fight in this war. The Bible actually uses the picture of a Roman soldier's armour to describe the resources he gives us. Paul advises:

> *Finally, be strong in the Lord and in his mighty power. Put on the whole armour of God so that you can take your stand against the devil's schemes (verses 10-11).*

You can read his description of this 'armour' in Ephesians 6:14-17. It has six pieces.

The belt of truth. The Roman soldier's belt was the thing that held all his armour together. For us this means that everything we do and all that we are hangs together on the fact that what God says is reality.

Allow the truth that God speaks to be the thing that holds your life together. This is your best protection against the Enemy's many attempts to deceive you.

The breastplate of righteousness. The soldier's breastplate allowed him to move into difficult situations knowing that arrows or spears could not pierce his heart. He was secure.

Our breastplate is righteousness—that is, the right way of living which flows from obedience to God and results in all things fitting together in his lovely way. When you live in the righteousness of God, you'll find yourself well protected from the Enemy's malicious attempts to twist things out of place.

It's important to see that you can't be righteous by your own efforts. Rather, God gives us *his* righteousness, through Jesus. So it's not a matter of us being perfect but of simply receiving this right way of living from him, and trusting him for the power to live it.

Feet fitted with the readiness that comes from the gospel of peace. The Roman soldier's boots enabled him to walk and move securely in all situations. The fact that God's good news is a message that says we don't have to have the mess we've got gives a growing security to move anywhere, at any time, with any people.

The shield of faith. The soldier's shield was made of leather

and soaked in water. Any burning arrows that hit it would go out. In exactly the same way, God's lovely gift of faith—the ability to trust and rely on him— enables us to defuse the hard attacks that come from the Enemy.

The helmet of salvation. A helmet protects the head, and God's rescue is something that holds our whole self—our spirit, mind, will, emotions and body—together.

The sword of the Spirit, which is the word of God.
Everything that God says is like a sharp sword that's very
effective. When he spoke at creation, the whole earth was
formed. When he speaks, things happen.

God's word cuts deep, and it's one of the most important
tools that the Spirit uses to teach and strengthen us. This
word comes to us through both the things he shows us in
Jesus, and the things he's said through his chosen
spokesmen. We find these two things in the Bible, which is
itself the word of God.

SALVATION—BEING MADE WHOLE

As we've seen earlier in this book, the word 'salvation'
primarily refers to the change God brings in our lives when
we are rescued from his anger at our disobedience and set
free from being controlled by the Enemy.

But this isn't the whole story. The word 'salvation' also
carries the idea of people being made really *whole*, in body,
soul and spirit. Salvation is an *ongoing* process of rescue and
making whole that will only be completed when Jesus
comes back again.

Paul makes it clear that salvation relies completely on
God's action. We start off as Christians by trusting him and
we keep on going in exactly the same way (Romans 1:17).
There's no room for anyone to feel they've achieved their
salvation in any way.

Paul sees salvation as something which is past, present
and future.

In the *past*, through what Jesus has done, we were
rescued from God's anger over our rebellion, from the
power of sin over us, and from the law (which simply
condemned us because we kept breaking it). This rescue is
now finished and complete. The moment you believed, you
were literally judged guilty and then forgiven. Christians

often call this 'justification', and we accept it for ourselves by faith.

In the *present*, God is at work through his Holy Spirit changing us into the people he wants us to be. It is his on-going, everyday action that gives us the power to live as Christians. We are called to cooperate with him in what he wants to do in us and to trust him to do it. (This present process is often called 'sanctification'.)

In the *future*, this process will come to a climax when God finishes his work by changing our old, dead bodies into wonderful, new spiritual bodies. This will happen in a moment—'in the twinkling of an eye' (1 Corinthians 15:52). Then we'll discover the full wonder and glory of being the person he made us to be—and that's why this event is often called 'glorification'. Once again, we trust God by faith to bring it about.

HOW YOU KNOW WHAT GOD WANTS

Many Christians ask the question: How do I know what God wants me to do? And they find a real conflict in themselves, because on the one hand they've always been taught to think carefully about things and plan them for themselves, but on the other hand they're now being told to listen to what God says.

> **Want to know more?**
> You can explore the full details of what God has done for you in salvation through books such as *Free Indeed* by Tom Marshall (published by Sovereign World) and *In Christ Jesus* by Colin Urquhart (published by Hodder and Stoughton). *Healing Adventure* by Anne White (Sovereign World) covers many of the ways God wants to work in our lives to transform us.

Some people get so confused they spend most of their lives *looking* for what God wants but rarely actually *doing* it.

It's important to remember at all times that God has made you a decisive person. That is, he's given you the free ability to make decisions that really matter. Following him doesn't ever mean sitting back and letting him run your life like a puppet. It always means listening to him and then being decisive in choosing to go his way.

Elsewhere in this book we've discussed some of the ways God speaks to us (see pages 47–53). But in listening to God, the starting point has to be your *attitude*. If you want to know what God wants you to do, it's important to have your mind made up that you're prepared to do whatever he says, when he says it.

When people have a desire to do what's godly, they'll usually find what God wants them to do. Then the best advice is that given by Jesus' mother to the servants at the wedding in Cana where he turned water into wine: 'Do whatever he tells you' (read the whole story in John 2:1-11).

God will often give you ideas which won't be things you've thought up yourself. When you have an idea that you think may be God speaking, it's important to always test it by asking:

- Is this idea something that sounds like God? (You'll need to read the Bible regularly to get to know what he's like.) If it's not consistent with the Bible or God's character, resist it (that is, refuse to accept it) in the name of Jesus.
- Does the idea fit the situation you're in? If it seems totally out of order, it's probably not from him. Again, resist it in the name of Jesus.
- Sometimes it's helpful to bounce the idea off another

Christian or group of Christians. Look for their confirmation that what you sense is from God.

If the idea stays after you've tested it, then trust that it is from God and ask him for wisdom to know what to do next. Be prepared to launch out and begin doing what he tells you to.

All the way along you need to stay alert. If you feel an uneasy sense that something isn't right, stop and check further, don't just rush on.

The important thing is that when you have a sense that you know what God wants, be prepared to begin. I have a friend who hates washing dishes, but one day she told me she'd discovered the key to getting them done: *start*. It's the same with knowing what God wants. When you have a bit of an idea, start—you'll be amazed how often the pieces fall into place.

As you move along, you'll often find that God will confirm the direction you're going in many ways—sometimes through other people, sometimes through circumstances, and always with a sense of 'rightness' in your own life.

WHAT'S ALL THIS ABOUT THE BLOOD OF JESUS?

Sometimes people hear other Christians talking about 'the blood of Jesus washing away our sin' and become a little confused about what his blood has to do with us.

The idea is based on a practice that God gave to the ancient Jewish people as a kind of picture to help them understand the way their sins could be forgiven. He told them that when they disobeyed him in different ways, they needed to respond by making an animal sacrifice that demonstrated their repentance.

Of course, if you sacrifice an animal there's always blood. And the blood being poured out on the altar in the Old Testament was a declaration of the fact that (1) the people were doing what God told them to do, and (2) he would do what he said he would, in forgiving them and restoring their fellowship with him.

When we come to the New Testament and we see that Jesus dies and his blood is spilt, the same idea of God's faithfulness and fullness is clear. The writer of the book of Hebrews says that Jesus' death is the *perfect* sacrifice for sin—the ultimate sacrifice of which all the animal sacrifices were merely pictures (see Hebrews 9:11-14).

> **Want to know more?**
> A useful general book on this and many other subjects is *The Lion Handbook to Christian Belief* (published by Lion Publishing).

So when people talk about 'applying the blood' to people's lives, they're talking about the fact that God's action in Jesus makes it possible for their complete renewing. More, it means that, in giving them this eternal newness, God is satisfied that things are working the way he said they should (in theological language we might say 'his righteousness is satisfied').

Going on with Jesus

By now, as you've read this book and begun living under God, I'm sure your life is already very different. Since the day you first responded to Jesus' love, many things would have happened—and some of them may well have blown your mind. Dealing with God is often like that. He's majestic and wonderful and awesome in every way.

What has been happening? You've been going through your 'birthing' as a new Christian. The next step, after surviving the initial birth process, is to grow. And much of that growing will occur in very ordinary, day-by-day living.

When a baby is born, there's a lot of celebration and joy. There's also a lot of care taken over its initial days in the outside world. Once the birth is complete and the baby has a firm grip on life, growing is a matter of going on a day at a

time—eating food, doing exercise, living within the context
of a family, learning to understand and speak language.
Through it all, the child gradually grows in wisdom and
knowledge of the person he or she is.

It's not unlike that with Christians. The beginning of
your new life often requires a lot of care: there are many
things to set right, important actions to take, new ideas to
reflect on. Then, as you move on, it becomes a matter of
gradually learning to be the person God made you to be in
the first place—a person who walks every day with him as
your friend, in a relationship with him that enables you to
grow to know him better and better.

Remember, Jesus said, 'I don't call you servants, I call
you friends; servants don't know their master's business,
but I've told you what God is on about' (see John 15:15).
You can now move on that way, knowing him as a living
friend.

Reading Christian books

As you continue in your Christian life, you'll no doubt come
across many books that Christians have written to deal with
various aspects of following Jesus. You may also come across
cassette tapes and videos.

We live in a day when almost anyone can write a book or
make a tape or video. This underlines for us the importance of
testing the things we read and see. Just because something is
written down or recorded doesn't necessarily mean it's true. We
need to carefully check everything we read and hear, for even
Christian brothers and sisters can sometimes lead us astray.

On page 52 I spoke about how to test the things people say
to make sure they're what God is saying. Similar tests apply in
reading a book or listening to a tape or video.

• Does what this person is saying agree with what God says
about himself in the Bible?

• Is it in keeping with the way other Christians have
understood things?

• Is there evidence in the life of the author that indicates the

Being Jesus' friend means that he will treat *you* as a friend. While he has a mind about what he wants, he never *demands* that you do it; he always leaves you free to choose. He will never give you a set of rules and say, 'If you dutifully keep these rules you'll be a good friend'. Rather he says, 'If you love me you'll do what I want'—out of the freedom of love, not compulsion.

What God wants for every Christian is to walk quietly on with him, choosing every day to live in a way that pleases him, and endeavouring, in the ordinariness of wherever they are, to live as people who belong to him and who obey him as their true ruler.

WHAT IF MY RELATIONSHIP WITH GOD SEEMS TO GRIND TO A HALT?

Almost certainly there will be times in the future when you will feel that your life or your relationship with God isn't

book was written from an experience of walking with God himself? And does what he's saying work in his life?

• Does this material free you to live as God wants? Or does it invite you to follow a particular technique or set of rules which effectively takes you away from the freedom that Christ died to give you?

Whenever you read a book or listen to a tape, you will almost certainly find that some things in it will be very helpful to you and some won't. Don't feel you have to accept everything; rather, ask God's Holy Spirit to give you insight to know the truth.

And never forget: while things like books, cassette tapes and videos can be lovely resources, they all pale into insignificance alongside the Bible, which is God's 'breathed' word where he's revealed himself and where Jesus is made known in the most clear way. And ultimately even the words of the Bible aren't the most important thing. The most important thing is God himself—the one we know as Saviour, King and Father.

getting anywhere. Most Christians experience this from time to time. If this happens there's one thing to remember: *no matter what, you can always come back to him.*

This is especially important when you sin against him. You know you're a person who deserves God's anger because you've disobeyed him, yet amazingly he's chosen to have mercy on you. So if you sin against him, always come back for forgiveness.

Even if you reach a point where you think things are pretty bad, the principle is: keep turning back to him. He'll never turn you away. He promises that.

Martin Luther, a famous German Christian who lived around 500 years ago, once talked about a drunk man riding a horse. He said the man would make progress as long as every time he fell off he got back on again. He may actually climb on the left side and fall off the right. But as long as he climbed back into the saddle he would slowly make progress.

Sometimes we can feel a bit like that. We feel as if we're not making it very well as a Christian. But as long as you keep going back to God and asking for his forgiveness—as long as you 'keep climbing back on the horse'—you'll find that his action towards you will lead you on, and enable you through his grace to know the wonderful way of living that he planned for his creation.

THROW THIS BOOK AWAY

As I said at the start, following Jesus is the most important thing that this world knows. If God has used this book to help you understand more about what knowing him means, that's something to thank him for.

But hopefully, after a while this book will become useless to you because the things that it introduces you to will take you further into your relationship with the King, and your relationship with the King will supersede everything ever written down.

One day, when he comes back again, you'll meet him

face to face, and even ideas about how you should relate to him won't matter any more. Only he will. What an amazing day that will be!

Power on, in the name of the Lord Jesus!

How to go about reading the Bible

 The Bible is a collection of writings by more than forty different people written over the best part of 2,000 years! This special resource will give you a framework in which to read it and fit all the pieces together.

As a Christian you need to enjoy God's love letter to you. To do so you need to read it with an expectation that God will speak to you through it. Now that you know the Author of the Book personally—he's your heavenly Father—you'll find great encouragement and instruction from the things written in its pages.

The Bible is divided into two sections—the Old Testament and the New Testament. The Old Testament was written before Jesus was born on earth. It tells how God has

dealt with people through history (in fact, history is
'*his*-story'.) The New Testament was written shortly after
Christ lived on earth, died and rose again from the dead.

The first four books of the New Testament (Matthew,
Mark, Luke and John) are called the gospels and give the
story of Jesus and his mission on earth ('gospel' means
'good news'). The next book, called the Acts of the Apostles,
tells how Jesus went back to be with God the Father and
how his disciples then carried on his work. Many of the
things God showed them are recorded in the rest of the
New Testament, in the form of letters written by Christian
leaders to the young churches of the first century.

GETTING AN OVERVIEW OF THE WHOLE BOOK

The whole of the Bible is one big rescue story—the story of
how God has acted to bring rebellious people back into
friendship with himself. To understand it well, it's good to
get an overview of what it says.

This is useful in two ways. First, it will help you
understand where each piece of the Bible fits into the total
picture. Secondly, it will help you understand where *you* fit
into God's picture today.

Think about it like this. We're all like the extras in a film.
The stars play the action and our job is to cooperate with
whatever they're doing. If the scene is set in a cafe where a
meal is being enjoyed by everyone, we won't sit crying.
We'll act in harmony with the main actors.

In our case, the main actor is God himself. And in order
to know what our part is today, we need to have a good
idea of what he's done in the past, what he's up to now and
what he will do in the future. Then we'll be able to
cooperate with him.

We get this information from the Bible.

In a book called *The Framework* (Sovereign World, 1991),
David Boan provides a sort of shorthand way to understand
how God's big actions throughout history relate together.

For this he uses a diagram representing six major events from the Bible.

Point 1: The original creation

The first big event was God's creation of the world and how he set it up to work (Genesis 1–2). When he made the world, everything was 'very good' (Genesis 1:31).

At that time, God made man and woman 'in his image' and set down for them the whole way they were to live. He gave them the starting points for every aspect of their life and relationships. They were to know and love each other and to rule over the earth in a way that was like God's own caring rule.

They were also given freedom to choose between many things. In the story in Genesis chapters 1–3, they were told they could eat fruit from any tree in the Garden where God had placed them.

But there were some areas that God said were 'no go' areas for them—some trees they were not to eat from.

One of the most important things we learn from this first Point is how significant we are as human beings. We are made as God's 'co-rulers' on the earth, and our decisions really matter.

Point 2: The Fall (diagram next page)

The second really important event was when man and woman decided, against God's desires, to move into the area where he said not to go—to take fruit from the tree that God labelled 'Don't Touch' (Genesis 3). In so doing, they

found themselves in conflict with God because they had
disobeyed him.

This made them rebels; and once rebellion has begun, it's
very difficult to stop. Man and woman, having been
deceived by Satan into disobeying God, found themselves
wanting to hide from God. No longer was their relationship
with him open and lovely.

From this point on, everyone who is born as a
descendent of Adam and Eve—and in the Bible's
understanding that means the whole human race—finds
themselves with an inherited self-centred rebellion against
God. We now find it far more normal to disobey God than
to obey him.

Point 3: God's first action of rescue—his work with the Jewish people.

Humankind's disobedience created such a block that it
made it impossible for people to know God the way they
had before the Fall. But God didn't abandon them. He acted

to give them a way of relating to him again that protected them from the full chaos that their rebellion would lead to.

His action at this point was focussed on the people of Israel, the Jews. He did two things for them: he gave them commandments, which outlined the right way of living before God; and sacrifices, which were his way of sustaining their relationship with him when commandments were broken.

Unfortunately, the Jewish people weren't very good at following God's instructions. He kept on speaking directly to them through men called 'prophets', but they kept on rebelling.

Yet all through this period (which is covered by the whole Old Testament), God demonstrated that he still intensely loved his rebellious people. More than that, he promised that some day a special person would come who would rescue them and enable them to truly live by his intentions. This promised person was known as 'the Messiah', which in Hebrew means 'the Chosen One'.

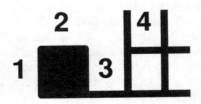

Point 4: The Chosen One arrives

Then one day, in what the Bible calls 'the fullness of time' (that is, when everything was exactly ready), God's Messiah, his special messenger, came on the earth. This was the greatest of all God's actions, because it was the sending of his own Son to rescue, not only the Jews, but all people.

This was the turning point of all history. Through his life, death and resurrection, Jesus smashed the reign of Satan and established God's reign on the earth in all those who obey him. The Bible calls this reign 'the Kingdom of God'.

Through his death and coming back to life again, he made it possible for people to be forgiven and to be given right standing with God.

Jesus also told us that one day he would return to the earth, and in the meantime he was going to send his Spirit to be with his children. Then he went back to be at the right hand of his Father, where he constantly looks after our interests.

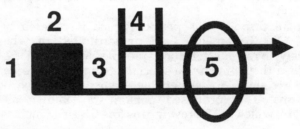

Point 5: Where we live now

Because of Jesus, God's Kingdom has broken out on the earth, and we can be part of it if we choose. Yet the old broken world keeps going on, and we have to live in it.

For those of us who follow Jesus, this means that life is always a kind of 'tension' between the old rebellious ways and the new ways of God's Kingdom. To follow Jesus always brings us into conflict with other things on the earth. It's like trying to live in two different kingdoms at once.

The Bible teaches us that this is a right tension to live in. We can't escape it. What we need to do is trust God for the power to live rightly in a messy world.

Jesus promises that we'll have his peace even while struggling with this difficult way of living. We need to face the fact of the tension realistically, but trust God to give us the ability we need to live in it at this present time.

This makes sense of the words of Jesus that he wants us

to live 'in' the world but not 'of' it (John 17:15-18). The world is *where* we live, but it doesn't shape our identity, values and behaviour. God does.

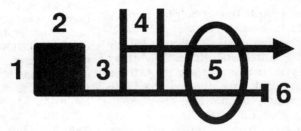

Point 6: The second coming of Jesus

The sixth great action of God is still in the future. It's when Jesus comes back again.

People will be absolutely amazed at his majesty and greatness, and everyone will bow before him awe-struck and overwhelmed. At his first coming his work was to rescue us; but at his return it will be to judge the world. Every human being is accountable to him.

Then the rebellious world will end and the reign of God and his Son, Jesus, will go on forever.

A READING GUIDE TO THE BIBLE

Within this framework, everything you come across in the Bible will fit somewhere. If you keep it in mind as you read, you'll find the different parts will come together more easily in your thinking.

It's important to make sure your Bible reading doesn't become too 'bitsy'—that is, reading here and there without any order. Another danger is to let it become an exercise where you rely more on notes that someone has written *about* the Bible than on the Bible itself.

A very helpful way of becoming a student of the whole Bible is to commit yourself to read as much as possible. Many people find that this means reading the whole Bible at

least every year. If you read three
chapters a day and five on Sunday,
you'll cover the entire Bible in one
year.

Some people find it helpful to have
a guide to help them stay on track.
Guides such as that developed by the
Scottish Christian Robert Murray
McCheyne many years ago can be
helpful. McCheyne divided the Bible
up over one year into four chapters to
be read each day. McCheyne's guide
is available from Banner of Truth
Trust, 3 Murrayfield Road, Edinburgh
EH12 6EL, United Kingdom.

Books about the Bible

There are many
books around
designed to help
people understand
the Bible, but two of
the most useful ones
are *The Lion
Handbook to the
Bible* and *The New
Bible Dictionary*
(published by
Inter-Varsity Press).

Being God's family together

 The relationships we have with other Christians are meant to be the source of great joy and love. This special resource will help you find a way ahead when they're not.

Anyone who has eaten a fruit salad knows how the distinctive taste that God has put in each fruit still comes through even when it's mixed up with other fruits. Every fruit stays itself even while it's contributing to the whole bowl.

That's what being God's people is like. In God's family there will always be diversity in our understanding of God's truth and in our experience of how God moves us. Like fruit in a fruit salad, we're called to live in that diversity. It is God's gift, and he takes great delight in it.

He also takes great delight in mixing all his diverse children into one great bowl—the church of Jesus.

In his letter to the Christians in Corinth, Paul paints a

word picture of the church as being like a Body with many parts (1 Corinthians 12, 13, 14). The Head is Jesus and each of us is a hand or a leg, an eye or an ear. We all have our parts to play under the leading of his Spirit. Being his family is very exciting (see box).

Paul recognizes that God deals with everyone individually. Within this God-given diversity, Christians are to live together in love, agreeing and working together for his glory. And where we disagree, we're to do so in a way that honours and cares for one another and so brings him glory, even though we don't see eye to eye. Paul writes:

> **The joy of being in God's family**
> Dietrich Bonhoeffer, a German Christian imprisoned and hanged for his opposition to Hitler, once said: 'The physical presence of other Christians is a source of incomparable joy and strength to the believer . . . the fellowship of Christian brethren is a gift of grace, a gift of the Kingdom of God.'

This love of which I speak is slow to lose patience—it looks for a way of being constructive. It is neither anxious to impress, nor does it cherish inflated ideas of its own importance . . . it is never rude . . . it never insists on its rights, is not quick to take offence and doesn't keep score of wrongs. It doesn't gloat over other men's sins but delights in the truth. Love knows no limit to its endurance, no end to its trust . . . (1 Corinthians 13, J. B. Phillips' translation).

CARVING UP THE BODY

Unfortunately, Christians often aren't very good at loving like this. We forget that diversity is God's gift. We disagree, relationships break down, and our love for one another—which God intends to be the thing that demonstrates to the world that we're really Jesus' disciples (John 13:34)—suffers.

When we divide the Body of Christ like this, it's like carving up a body with a meat cleaver.

Often we think that what causes division is our disagreement over doctrines or spiritual gifts or some other thing. But it's not. It's always our failure to love one another as we should.

Splits between Christians often have long histories of pride, harsh judgment of others, failure to listen and unwillingness to forgive. Lack of love grows into resentment, bitterness and sometimes hate.

The Body of Christ is broken, and the Spirit of God is saddened (Ephesians 4:30).

'TRADITIONS OF MEN'

It's also true that as humans we tend to move into tomorrow with our minds clearly fixed on what happened yesterday. We're like the man who insisted on driving forwards with his eyes glued to the rear vision mirror instead of the road ahead.

But God calls us clearly not to build up traditions that are 'made by men'. Jesus told the Jews that they had actually followed their human traditions rather than what God wanted from them. That could equally be said of many parts of God's church today (see box).

In reality there is only one church. It's made up of everyone who has the Spirit of Christ living in their hearts. But because of people's disagreements over the centuries, many small

> **Jesus critiques the 'traditions of men'**
> 'So the Pharisees and teachers of the law asked Jesus, "Why don't your disciples live according to the tradition of the elders instead of eating their food with 'unclean' hands?" He replied, "Isaiah was right when he prophesied about you hypocrites; as it is written: 'These people honour me with their lips, but their hearts are far from me. They worship me in vain, their teachings are but rules taught by men.' You have let go of the commands of God and are holding to the traditions of men" ' (Mark 7:5-8).

segments and divisions have grown up among God's
people.

What we need to see is that we are all part of *God's*
church, and we should let nothing stand in the way of being
his people first and only. Make no commitment apart from
the commitment to Jesus alone.

Effectively this means that, if we actually live in
dependence on Jesus and put aside our human traditions,
we will live in *inter*-dependence with every Christian who
ever comes along—even the ones we don't like—because
we'll have something that's absolutely in common with
them.

HOW TO BE ONE IN LOVE

Jesus' assumption (as shown in his prayer for his followers'
unity in John 17) is that, if we are submitted to the Master,
differences can be ironed out. If it is true that God has
joined us together in a Body, our expectation should be that
we'll be able to live practically on that basis.

When we do things his way, we can.

How is the church to be one in love? If we rely on human
processes alone to keep us together, we won't differ from
the local Rotary Club—and possibly won't operate as well!

But God has promised to grow in us the very attitudes
we need: the 'fruit of the Spirit' that Paul describes in
Galatians 5. Without love, joy, peace, patience, kindness,
goodness, faithfulness, gentleness and self-control, there can
be no real spiritual unity.

We can't make these fruit happen; God grows them in
us. But we must chose to live by the fruit he grows. This
involves refusing (as Paul puts it) to 'gratify the desires of
the sinful nature'. Among these are hatred, discord,
jealousy, rage, selfish ambition, dissension, envy, conceit,
provocation—all the monsters that rear their ugly heads
when Christians divide.

God calls us to build each other up, to care for each
other, and to submit to each other under Christ. In short, he

wants us to cooperate with him in building his church, not to be vandals!

> *Love must be sincere. Hate what is evil; cling to what*
> *is good. Be devoted to one another in brotherly love.*
> *Honour one another above yourselves (Romans*
> *12:9-10).*

UNITY—GOD CREATES IT, WE LIVE IT

Why should we be so concerned about being one in love? Because unity—the unity of 'all things in heaven and earth together under one head, Christ' (Ephesians 1:10)—is what God is ultimately on about!

In Ephesians, the apostle Paul shows that this ultimate unity of all things is to be seen now, in a kind of microcosm, in the church. This makes our unity very important indeed.

But this doesn't mean it's something we achieve by programs or organisation. God isn't interested in outward shows! In ancient times, Jewish people used to rip their clothes to show their sorrow for sin; but it was easy to go through the motions without truly repenting. The prophet Joel said, 'Rend your heart and not your garment' (Joel 2:13). God is interested in real change.

Joel goes on to encourage the Jewish priests to weep before God and plead with him to spare his people from judgment, because if they suffer, other nations will be able to point the finger and say, 'Where is their God?' (Joel 2:17-18).

Many non-Christians are asking that question of today's church. If those closest to us—our families, friends, neighbours—don't see evidence of God's truth working in our lives, we must question the reality of the words we speak in church.

God wants his church to keep growing, not through the latest marketing techniques, but through people being attracted to his work in us. When we allow the deep spiritual reality of our unity as his children to impact our lives, that's exactly what happens.

THE ANSWER TO DIVISION

Real change requires real power. But that power is not self-generated human power. It's the power of God's Spirit (see Zechariah 4:6).

As we saw in Section Five, God provides this power for building his church through certain supernatural tools—the gifts of the Spirit (see page 102). All these gifts are available for people to use, operating under the umbrella of the gifts of wisdom and faith and the fruit of love.

He stresses again and again that the bottom line is that people learn to rely on him for this power.

One of the Enemy's most cynical ploys is to foster division at precisely the point where God makes his power available. He ferments trouble over these gifts. The temptation for those who consciously use spiritual gifts to look down on those who do not—and vice versa—needs to be strongly resisted.

What is true for disagreement over spiritual gifts is true for all disagreements between Christians. James' analysis is still accurate:

> *What causes fights and quarrels among you? Don't they come from your desires that battle within you? (James 4:1-2)*

The answer to division is
- to humbly submit ourselves to God and one another;
- to resist the devil (who operates powerfully through unforgiveness, as 2 Corinthians 2:5-11 makes clear);
- to be anxious to know where *we* might be sinning in a situation; and
- to open ourselves to God to be changed.

Then we can be the worshipping, serving community he wants the world to see.

Like the first Christians, we need to throw off every sin that entangles us (Hebrews 12:1), lay aside the hurts we do to one another and renounce the pride, unforgiveness, haughty professionalism and traditionalism that weighs us down.

In place of these we are to fix our eyes on Jesus and become a people dependent on him, recognising him as the source of our being and relying on him for all our resources.

When we are dependent on him, we will find we need to be interdependent on each other.

LEADING AND FOLLOWING
One of the difficulties we have in maintaining our unity with other Christians is our modern attitude to authority. Most people today are not good followers.

It's not just that the people who are trusted with leadership tasks often don't know how to fulfil them. It's that the rest of us won't *let* them fulfil them!

So we talk behind our pastor's back instead of going to him. Or we send an eight page letter to our Bible study leader that clouts him over the head. In his hurt, he responds by digging his heels in. In the process, everybody sins.

The sort of politicking and lobbying that marks many twentieth century churches is quite different from the process Jesus himself laid down for dealing with differences—a process of lovingly setting things right (see Matthew 18:15-20; 5:23-24).

One problem we have is that we've made the mistake of believing leaders somehow have a special status. They don't. All of us are one together in the Body.

So what then is a leader? A leader is simply someone who serves the rest of us by doing a particular task. And what is a follower? A follower is someone who says, 'I'm prepared to trust God to lead us through that person'.

But instead we tend to say, 'We'll trust God to lead us through them until they start to lead us where we don't want to go. Then we will refuse to consider submission a viable option and will criticize them, refuse to cooperate with them, withdraw and attempt to deflect them from the direction they think God is saying we should go.'

The New Testament ethos of mutual submission under Christ is quite different, as we saw in Section Four ('When Christians Disagree', page 85).

But what if the leader is a bad leader, not teaching what the Bible teaches? I believe that Peter's response to that question would be the same as his response to the dilemma of Christian wives with unbelieving husbands:

> Wives . . . be submitted to your husbands so that, if
> any of them do not believe the word, they may be won
> over without talk by the behaviour of their wives,
> when they see the purity and reverence of your lives (1
> Peter 3:1-2).

Of course, it's also true that people in any kind of authority are called to be responsible, serving those they are leading in truth and love. All who lead will be judged by God for their leadership—especially those who teach the faith (James 3:1).

Submission to leadership, then, doesn't mean being docile and passive. No one should accept what a leader says simply because he's a leader! We all need to test what anyone says against the Scriptures, using our 'renewed minds' to sort truth from error on the basis of God's revelation (Romans 12:2).

But this testing must be done in submission.

Practically this means that where you feel leaders have got off track, you should feed back to them lovingly and gently. They in turn should listen, for you may be the voice of God to them.

OUR TRUE LEADER
Ultimately, we have only one Leader: Jesus. *He* is our Lord.

Any human leader among God's people must never forget that he or she is only doing a task, and must never try to control others. That would be taking over Jesus' place as Lord in their lives!

Be especially careful of leaders who ask you to obey them or who show evidence that they want to control you—including showing a strong interest in the money you might contribute. As I have said often in this book, God is gentle, holy, righteous and just, and servant-leaders who are obeying him will lead in a way that demonstrates the same spirit.

God's 'no go' areas

IIII➤ There are some areas of life into which God says 'don't go'—especially occult activities and beliefs. Even small involvements can stain us and imprison us. This resource shows how to experience God's freedom.

Ask any lifesaver: it's vital that swimmers recognize the importance of choosing to swim between the flags on the beach. These flags indicate the area that is constantly patrolled and therefore safe to swim in. People can choose to swim outside the flags, but if they do they move out of safety.

There may or may not be visual evidence of the dangers, but those who know the beach direct swimmers away from the perils for their own good. Only a disobedient or foolish person would ignore the flags and move into the dangerous 'no-go' areas outside them.

God, who, as Creator and Owner of everything, knows

all things and has the right to say what should be in His
world, says that *he* has some 'no go' areas, too. To move into
them is to disobey him and to put ourselves in great danger.

As we saw right back in Section One, when God placed
man and woman in the garden of Eden, he commanded
them to take authority as responsible rulers on the earth and
to eat from any of the trees in the garden, with one
exception. If they did eat from that out-of-bounds tree, they
would die (see Genesis 2:16-17.)

This shows that right at the beginning there were some
'no go' areas which God, for his own good reasons,
prohibited the man and woman from entering. Satan's
method of tempting Adam and Eve was to deceive them
into believing that this command from God, rather than
protecting them, actually robbed them of their potential to
fully enjoy God's world (see Genesis 3:4-5).

As soon as they disobeyed and ate from the prohibited
tree, they discovered that God's command had been for
their good. Their action placed them in unbelievable
jeopardy. In fact, it ushered death into human experience
and condemned all humankind after them to following a
path of disobedient rebellion against God.

They moved outside the flags, and all of us have been
suffering the consequences ever since.

God hasn't changed. There are still areas which he tells
us not to have any contact with whatsoever, for our own
good. But often the very fact that God says 'don't go there'
creates a fascination in rebellious people.

Among the most serious of these 'no go' areas is what we
often talk about today as 'the occult'. The word 'occult'
simply means 'hidden' or 'secret' things—that is, things
God has given us no information about and which he says
it's not right for us to inquire into ourselves.

A LITTLE DABBLE WON'T HURT . . .
Even if we only have a little to do with these occult areas,

we give Satan a way in which he can control us and take us into other areas of disobedience.

Paul told the Roman Christians that they would be the slaves of whatever they obeyed (see Romans 6:11-16). In other words, if you choose to obey sin, it will enslave you. He said:

> Do not offer parts of your body to sin, as instruments
> of wickedness, but rather offer yourselves to God
> (Romans 6:13).

It's easy for people to get caught up in occult activities which in the end rob them of the freedom to be the person God meant them to be. This is both dreadfully damaging to them and, more importantly, disobedient and offensive to God.

So where exactly is it that God says 'don't go' into these areas? In many places in the Bible.

When God took the people of Israel into the Promised Land, he said to them:

> When you enter the land the Lord your God is giving
> you, do not learn to imitate the detestable ways of the
> nations there. Let no one be found among you who
> sacrifices his son or daughter in the fire, who practices
> divination or sorcery, interprets omens, engages in
> witchcraft, or casts spells, or who is a medium or
> spiritist or who consults the dead. Anyone who does
> these things is detestable to the Lord, and because of
> these detestable practices the Lord your God will drive
> out those nations before you. You must be blameless
> before the Lord your God (Deuteronomy 18:9-13).

The Israelites responded:

> The secret things belong to the Lord our God, but the
> things revealed belong to us and to our children

> *forever, that we may follow all the words of [God's]*
> *law (Deuteronomy 29:29).*

Later, in the New Testament, Paul put it this way:

> *The acts of the sinful nature are obvious: sexual*
> *immorality, impurity and debauchery; idolatry and*
> *witchcraft; hatred, discord, jealousy, fits of rage,*
> *selfish ambition, dissensions, factions and envy;*
> *drunkenness, orgies, and the like. I warn you, as I did*
> *before, that those who live like this will not inherit the*
> *Kingdom of God (Galatians 5:19-21).*

HOW TO CLEAN UP YOUR LIFE

Check your own life for any places where you have been
involved in any of these occult 'no go' areas. The list
starting on the next page will help you.

As you read it through, ask God to show you things that
you need to claim his forgiveness for. Don't assume that
something is a problem for you just because it's on the list;
trust the Holy Spirit to show you what *he* wants you to deal
with.

All these areas are very significant. You may be tempted
to think that some are trivial or that you can dismiss them
because you did them for fun or out of curiosity rather than
'seriously'. But your motive doesn't matter. Any
involvement has taken you into places where God says
'don't go', and for that you need his forgiveness.

If you have done any of these things—whether
frequently or just once, whether as an adult or a child—take
the following action:

- repent carefully and specifically for all the deeds the
  Holy Spirit shows you that you've done;
- claim God's forgiveness and cleansing, and believe
  you have them (he gives them freely for even the most
  vile sins);

• firmly renounce each sin and involvement (that is, decisively turn away from it).

(Refer back to page 45 if you want to remind yourself of the way God has given us to deal with sin.)

It's a good idea to read the list slowly, taking time to let the Holy Spirit point things out to you. One of the Enemy's tricks is to get you to rush through so you miss important things.

1. Have you ever:

☐ broken God's first commandment (Exodus 20:3: 'You shall have no other gods before me') by worshipping or praying to other 'gods'?

☐ inquired about other 'gods'—even for fun or for a course at school or university? Have you voluntarily searched out information about other religions even though God has said not to?

☐ visited places where so-called 'gods' (which are really demons in disguise) are worshipped? This includes pagan temples anywhere in the world, even native 'sacred sites' or ceremonies. (The reason for your visit may have been to join the worship, or it may have been under the guise of tourism, the study of architecture or history, photography or simply personal fascination. The key question is: Did you have Kingdom business there, or was it just curiosity?)

☐ voluntarily inquired into Islam, Hinduism or any other non-Christian beliefs? (Obviously if you meet a Hindu person and God calls you to talk with them, then you are under his protection. What you learn in serving the King doesn't affect you.)

☐ owned any occult or pagan religious objects? There may be curses on them. (After asking God's forgiveness, it's a good idea to destroy them. See the example in Acts 19:17-20.)

☐ searched for truth without basing your search on the person of Christ? He said, 'I am the way, the truth and the life' (John 14:6).

☐ blasphemed or mocked God?

☐ denied the central realities about Jesus: the fact He is both God and Man; the fact that His death is the only thing that can make you right with God; the fact that He rose bodily from the grave; the fact that He is coming again to judge the earth?

☐ been involved in meditation or yoga?

☐ been involved with non-Christian religious sects?

☐ been involved in Satan worship or associated activities?

☐ participated in spiritism or seances?

☐ used a ouija board, crystal ball or other device to contact spirits?

☐ been involved in psychography (writing controlled by spirits or 'photography' of spirits)?

☐ consulted a medium or had your fortune told by use of cards, tea leaves, palm reading or some other method?

☐ spoken to the dead, or prayed to Mary or the saints (who were only ordinary human beings and can't now be prayed to)?

☐ participated in necromancy (gaining information or doing magic through communication with the dead) or in sexual intercourse with an incubus (demonic spirit)?

☐ read or listened to horoscopes (even for fun)?

☐ had a 'life reading' made, or believed in or considered reincarnation?

☐ had your life analysed according to biorhythms, numerology or your handwriting?

☐ been involved in mind science (the idea that 'mind' is the only reality and that physical matter, sickness, suffering and sin are not real)?

☐ practised divining (attempting to discover things that are obscure or future by some occult means)? This includes water divining.

☐ been involved in 'rebirthing' (supposedly being taken back into your pre-birth life, which is actually impossible)?

☐ made a blood pact?

☐ put a hex or curse on anyone, or cast a magic spell?

☐ wished that you were dead or that someone else was dead? (To wish this is to commit your will to agree with Satan to destroy you. For a Christian it can bring serious 'double-mindedness'—that is, a conflict between the desire for life that God gives you and the desire for death that you have previously committed to.)

☐ practised mind-control, mental suggestion, telepathy or extra-sensory perception (ESP)?

☐ engaged in practices such as astral travel or levitation?

☐ owned or read material (books, tapes, records, videos) on occult, magical, spiritualist or pornographic subjects?

☐ taken 'mind-expanding' drugs?

☐ blanked your mind out for any reason, including art or drama? (God intends your mind to be the tool you use to check for truth (Romans 12:2), so blanking it out is very dangerous.)

☐ been hypnotized or performed self-hypnosis? (Hypnosis involves a degree of putting your mind under another person, rather than under Christ alone.)

☐ chanted a mantra—even the name 'Jesus'?

☐ been involved in witchcraft (whether 'white' or 'black')?

☐ used a charm for luck or protection?

☐ passed on a chain letter out of fear?

☐ subscribed to superstitions—throwing salt over your shoulder, wishing on a star, fear of black cats or Friday the 13th, etc?

☐ joined a secret society?

☐ watched any of these things on TV, video or movies—including 'innocent' programs such as comedies about witches, ghosts or genies? (Again, the point is that you have voluntarily taken in 'occult' information—even if you laughed at it. Many of these programs and films blatantly mock God.)*

* This list isn't complete and the Holy Spirit may bring other things to your attention that aren't named here. Deal with them, too!

2. Are you free?

Are there any areas of your life where you are not free to stop behaving in a way you know isn't right? Any habit or involvement which you've never told anyone else about will quite possibly be an area where you lack God's freedom.

These things can be like prisons: prisons of rebellion, fear, disappointment, control, unbelief, double-mindedness, independence, self-pity, resentment, lust, pride, insecurity, despair, gluttony, ambition, 'religiosity' and more.

If this is your experience, repent of the sin concerned and ask God to set you free. You may need to ask another Christian to pray with you about these matters.

3. Are you fully committed to Jesus?

Check to see that nothing holds your obedience other that Jesus. If there are areas of your life where you aren't obeying Him, repent and give each individual area to Him. Then you will be free to obey God and nothing else.

Commit yourself to stay free. Remember: God makes you free to do anything which doesn't rob you of your freedom!

4. Watch that pride!

Check to ensure that you have given no place to pride, for pride robs God of His rightful glory. If the Holy Spirit convicts you in this area, repent and commit yourself to live humbly and faithfully.

Word list

 There are many words that Christians use
which you may not be familiar with. This
list is not complete but includes some of
the more common words. A helpful book
that gives many more is *The Lion
Concise Bible Encyclopaedia*. (Note:
words used in definitions that are
themselves explained elsewhere in the
list are marked with an *.)

adore, adoration
Expressing to God the wonder, excitement and awe we feel
when we recognize who he is and what he's done. (See page
43.)

agnostic
A person who does not know, or who thinks it is impossible
to know, whether there is a God.

angel
A messenger of God. A created being familiar with him face
to face, therefore of an order of created beings higher than
that of humankind.

apostle
This is a Greek word that has been written in English letters. It means a 'sent one', a messenger. Jesus' original twelve disciples*, along with Paul and others, are called apostles in the New Testament.

ascension
The time when Jesus returned to his Father after being on earth. He now sits beside the Father to intercede* for us.

atheist
A person who believes that there is no God.

atone, atonement
This word means 'at-one-ment'. It speaks of the work of Jesus in dealing with people's sin* and restoring their relationship with God—making them 'at one' with him again.

baptize
This is a Greek word that has been written in English letters. Basically it means to be 'immersed' or 'washed'. Christians use the word in two areas.

Being baptized in water is an action of obedience to God which speaks of how He washes away our sin* and how the Holy Spirit* renews our spirit*. It is therefore understood as a sign of initiation into God's family. (See page 31.)

Jesus told his disciples* that they would also be baptized in the Holy Spirit. He meant that the Holy Spirit would come and, at the believer's invitation, would immerse them in himself so that they would know power and ability for living and service. (See page 32–33, 97–103.)

breaking bread
An early Christian way of referring to what Christians today often call the Lord's Supper or communion*.

charismata
This Greek word is usually translated 'spiritual gifts'. It is based on the word for grace (*charis*), so it more accurately

means 'grace gifts'. It refers to special abilities and powers given freely by God to his people. (See pages 102–103.)

Christ
The Greek form of the Hebrew word Messiah*.

church
The Greek word translated 'church' refers to the gathering of people who have been made part of God's family. The church is Christ's 'body' and He alone is 'Head'. In the New Testament this word is never used of a building! There is only one church of Jesus Christ, but it gathers in many different geographical locations. (See pages 53 and 127–135.)

communion
This word means sharing in something with someone. It is often used of the Lord's Supper, where Christians eat bread and drink wine or grape juice to remember Jesus' death for them.

compassion
A divine as well as a human quality that is really love expressed as mercy and pity.

confession
'To confess' means to agree with someone. Christians use this word to mean agreeing with God when he shows them how they have sinned. They agree with Him that their guilt is real and that they need to be forgiven (see pages 44–45). They also use it to refer to agreeing with God about who Jesus is and that he's their Lord—hence 'confess' can mean 'declare to others your personal relationship and allegiance to God'.

conversion
A turning or returning to something. In the case of Christians, a turning to God.

covenant
A solemn and binding undertaking to do something or get something done. For the Christian, God has made two

outstanding covenants: first, that he would be with the Jewish people and would make them a great nation; secondly, that through Jesus, a Jewish man, he would rescue and redeem* people from *every* nation. The covenants that God makes with humankind are all based on his trustworthiness and love.

crucify
Put to death by nailing to a cross (as Jesus was). Also, a picture of how God wants us to 'die' to our selfishness and live by his Holy Spirit*.

deacon
This is an English word taken from a Greek term that means 'one who serves'. Many Christians have understood certain people who take authority in local churches as 'deacons'.

demon
An evil spirit—literally, a 'little devil'.

discern
To perceive something, or to distinguish between two things.

disciple
A follower. One who adheres to the teaching of someone else and models their life on that person.

elder
A more mature person who is recognized as godly in life and action and is given authority in the local church to lead and care for God's people.

epistle
A written communication, a letter.

eternity
A realm of being which is beyond time and not influenced by it. God is in eternity and one day we will be with him there. When a person turns to Jesus, the Bible says they receive 'eternal life'—a quality of life now that gives them a

limited but still wonderful taste of what eternity will be like with him.

evangelism
To announce the good news about Jesus to other people. (See pages 61–62.)

faith
The ability given by God which enables people to have confidence and trust about things they cannot see if they only use their human senses. For the Christian it is often used of reliance on God. It is not a leap in the dark but a believing in God's trustworthiness.

Fall (the)
'The Fall' speaks of that time when man and woman disobeyed God, so that their relationship with him—and consequently their relationship with the whole of the created order—was broken. This has repercussions for every person from that time on.

glorify
To worship*, to praise, to lift up for all to see.

glorification
Christians use this word to describe the way that we will finally be when God has finished his work of transforming us and we meet him face to face. It is one aspect of being saved*. Like justification* and sanctification*, glorification is something done to us by God. It is his work alone. (See pages 107–108.)

godly
What pleases God and is consistent with his character.

grace
The Bible teaches that God loves us and is kind and good to people. We do not deserve this. God's action is seen as his 'grace'. Often described as 'undeserved favour'.

holy
This word means whole, healed, entire, unimpaired, complete. In relation to God, it is used to speak of the fact that he is truth and is absolutely complete and pure and needs nothing. (See page 27.)

holiness
The way God wants us to live, reflecting his lovely character.

Holy Spirit
The third person of the Trinity*. He is God interacting with us. (See pages 97–98.)

humanism
Any view of life that begins with people alone and ignores God.

Immanuel
A name for Jesus that literally means 'God is with us'.

incarnation
To be in a human body (as when Jesus came to earth).

intercede, intercession
Asking God to act on behalf of others. (See pages 46–47.)

justification
God saying to us: 'You are guilty and deserve punishment for your rebellion against me, yet I forgive you because Jesus took the punishment you deserve.' It is one aspect of being saved*. Like glorification* and sanctification*, justification is something done to us by God. It is his work alone. (See pages 19, 107.)

kingdom of God (the)
This is not a geographical location but refers to God's kingly rule in the lives of the people who obey him. Wherever men and women obey him, there he rules as king.

law
When Christians speak of 'the law' they are referring to the law that was given to the people of Israel by God to keep them from chaos. (This law was never meant to be rules that would enable people to get to know God; rather, it was intended to show people who already knew him how to live in the way he wanted.)

Lord's Supper (the)
See 'communion'.

majesty
We refer to someone who is kingly and dignified and who deserves honour and esteem as 'majestic'. To recognize someone's majesty means to respect the excellence, greatness and beauty of that person.

Messiah
A name for Jesus that literally means 'God's specially chosen and promised One'.

occult
Literally means 'covered' or 'hidden', but used today to refer to things of supernatural evil. Occult things are primarily places which God has kept hidden from us. They are God's 'no go' areas. (See pages 27–28 and Special Resource 3.)

parables
Stories Jesus used to explain the nature of God's Kingdom. To some people they were quite confusing, but when God helped people understand them they became very clear.

Passover
A Jewish celebration remembering the time when God rescued the Israelite people from slavery in Egypt.

Pentecost
For Jews, the fiftieth day after the Passover*. For Christians, also the time when the Holy Spirit* was first poured out on Jesus' disciples*.

personal relationship with God
God takes no delight in 'religion' but really wants to call us back into the relationship with himself that he intended us to have when he first made us. This is a spiritual relationship in which we can listen to and talk with him and know and obey him.

prayer
Talking with God. (See pages 42–47.)

prophecy
God's clear word spoken through people in specific situations. Sometimes this includes predicting things that will happen in the future.

prophet
One whom God uses to bring prophetic messages.

propitiation
A word used to describe the way God gave Jesus as a payment to make it possible for him to no longer be angry with us.

reconciliation
To bring two people who have been enemies back together. Used particularly to refer to God and people being brought back together.

redeem, redemption
A word used to describe Jesus' action in buying back freedom for those who have been enslaved by sin*.

repent, repentance
Turning away from rebellion and sin* and turning to God.

resurrection
God bringing Jesus back to life after he'd been killed.

revelation
A word coming from the word 'reveal' and used to refer to God making himself known. Also, the name of the last book in the Bible.

sacrifice
A voluntary offering to God. For the Jews, sacrifices of animals were the way God gave them to atone* for their sins*, and this became a picture of the way the sacrifice of Jesus would deal with the sins of the entire world.

sacrament
A physical ritual that corresponds to the spiritual reality of God's action. Used by some Christians to refer to the two actions of obedience that Jesus asked of his people: baptism* and breaking bread whenever they meet (also known as the Lord's Supper or communion*).

salvation, being saved
God's action in rescuing us from the consequences of our rebellion and remaking us into people like Jesus.

sanctification
God's ongoing action of transforming us into the people he wants us to be. It is one aspect of being saved*. Like justification* and glorification*, sanctification is something done to us by God. It is his work alone. (See page 107.)

Satan
'Satan' is the Hebrew name and 'devil' is the Greek name for a spiritual being who is evil and opposed to God. (See pages 73, 103–106.)

second coming
The time when Jesus Christ will return to the earth and judge all people.

sin
Sin is described in different ways in the Bible: as rebellion against God, missing God's mark, disobeying God's

commands. Sin always results in people losing the freedom
God meant them to know. (See page 15.)

soul
That aspect of us as people where we *think* and
discriminate, *decide* about our actions and *feel* the outcomes
of the working of our spirit*, soul and body. Some
Christians speak about these functions as the mind, the will
and the emotions. (See pages 34–35.)

sovereignty
To be sovereign means to hold and exercise supreme rule.
God is sovereign over the entire universe.

speaking in tongues
A gift given by God through his Holy Spirit* which enables
us to speak to Him in words of a language which we have
never learned. This is our spirit* communicating with His
Spirit. (See page 34.)

spirit
That aspect of us as people where we commune with God
and where we experience that deep sense of knowing where
we really 'own' the things that we hear. Also, the place
where our conscience knows what is good. (See pages
34–35.)

temptation
This word literally means 'testing'. Christians normally use
it to refer to Satan's* attempts to lead people into sin*.
Temptation itself is not sin; giving in to it is.

Trinity
Although not used in the Bible, this is a word Christians
have traditionally used to describe God. While God is
obviously much greater than we can fully understand, we
know him by the way he acts toward us as a Father, a
saviour Son and the Holy Spirit*. He is all three, but all the
time we know he is one God. (See pages 93–94.)

ungodly
What displeases God and is quite opposite to his character.

word of knowledge
A gift that God gives through his Holy Spirit* which enables people to have knowledge they could not possibly otherwise have about some person or situation. This knowledge enables them to help their brothers and sisters in godly* ways.

word of wisdom
A gift that God gives through his Holy Spirit* which enables people to have the wisdom they need to decide and act in ways that please Him.

worship
To give God the honour he deserves, both in the things we say and the things we do.

wrath
God's justified anger when people don't acknowledge him and instead direct their worship to other things.